Prioritizing Security Cooperation with Highly Capable U.S. Allies

Framing Army-to-Army Partnerships

ANGELA O'MAHONY, DAVID E. THALER, BETH GRILL,
JENNIFER D. P. MORONEY, JASON H. CAMPBELL, RACHEL TECOTT,
MARY KATE ADGIE

Prepared for the United States Army
Approved for public release; distribution unlimited

 ARROYO CENTER

For more information on this publication, visit **www.rand.org/t/RRA641-1**.

About RAND

The RAND Corporation is a research organization that develops solutions to public policy challenges to help make communities throughout the world safer and more secure, healthier and more prosperous. RAND is nonprofit, nonpartisan, and committed to the public interest. To learn more about RAND, visit www.rand.org.

Research Integrity

Our mission to help improve policy and decisionmaking through research and analysis is enabled through our core values of quality and objectivity and our unwavering commitment to the highest level of integrity and ethical behavior. To help ensure our research and analysis are rigorous, objective, and nonpartisan, we subject our research publications to a robust and exacting quality-assurance process; avoid both the appearance and reality of financial and other conflicts of interest through staff training, project screening, and a policy of mandatory disclosure; and pursue transparency in our research engagements through our commitment to the open publication of our research findings and recommendations, disclosure of the source of funding of published research, and policies to ensure intellectual independence. For more information, visit www.rand.org/about/principles.

RAND's publications do not necessarily reflect the opinions of its research clients and sponsors.

About This Report

This report documents research and analysis conducted as part of a project entitled *Prioritizing U.S. Army Security Cooperation with Allies in Support of Operation Inherent Resolve and Operation Freedom's Sentinel*, sponsored by the Office of the Deputy Chief of Staff, G-35/7, U.S. Army. The purpose of the project was to help prioritize Army security cooperation activities with highly capable allies to improve interoperability and coalition support as part of Operation Inherent Resolve and Operation Freedom's Sentinel, which includes U.S. engagement with NATO's Operation Resolute Support.

This research was conducted within RAND Arroyo Center's Strategy, Doctrine, and Resources Program. RAND Arroyo Center, part of the RAND Corporation, is a federally funded research and development center (FFRDC) sponsored by the United States Army.

RAND operates under a "Federal-Wide Assurance" (FWA00003425) and complies with the *Code of Federal Regulations for the Protection of Human Subjects Under United States Law* (45 CFR 46), also known as "the Common Rule," as well as with the implementation guidance set forth in U.S. Department of Defense Instruction 3216.02. As applicable, this compliance includes reviews and approvals by RAND's Institutional Review Board (the Human Subjects Protection Committee) and by the U.S. Army. The views of sources utilized in this study are solely their own and do not represent the official policy or position of the U.S. Department of Defense or the U.S. Government.

Acknowledgments

We would like to thank MG Bradley Gericke and MG Christopher McPadden (Ret.) and the Office of the Deputy Chief of Staff, G-35/7, U.S. Army for sponsoring the project and COL Rob Howieson, Headquarters, Department of the Army (HQDA) G-35-SSC division chief, for his support, guidance and feedback throughout the project. We thank Robert Maginnis and LTC Patrick Blankenship in HQDA G-35-SSC and Michael Prater in the Deputy Assistant Secretary for Defense Exports and Cooperation office for their ongoing engagement in this study. We received great support from the British Embassy in the United States and particularly would like to thank military attaché Brigadier Paul Tennant, assistant military attaché COL Paul Bates, and MAJ Paul Young, SO2 G2/G3. We thank key officials from Australia's Department of Defence, Department of Foreign Affairs and Trade, and the Office of National Assessments, as well as numerous colleagues from RAND Australia, the Australian National University, and the Australian Strategic Policy Institute. We appreciate the great support and contributions of RAND colleagues Jennifer Kavanagh, Stephen Watts, and Dylan Nir.

Finally, we wish to thank the two technical reviewers of the draft report, Tommy Ross from the Center for Strategic and International Studies and our RAND colleague Mike McNerney, for their comments and recommendations. Their insightful reviews greatly strengthened the substance of the report.

Summary

The U.S. strategic security environment has undergone a shift during the past decade: The regional focus on countering violent extremist organizations has given way to long-term global competition against near-peer adversaries Russia and China. Security cooperation (SC), especially with our closest, most capable (*highly capable*) allies, is emphasized as a high-priority tool for pursuing an extensive array of overlapping national interests.[1] The United States and its allies recognize that, in a time of increasing requirements and limited resources, they must work in coalitions and engage regional stakeholders by bringing different strengths and perspectives to combined efforts. However, recent operations and efforts suggest that more can be done to create and sustain the mechanisms that increase the effectiveness of joint activities.

In this report, we present methods to enable the U.S. Army to better prioritize and coordinate its SC activities with those activities pursued by its allies and partners, allowing it to meet its assigned objectives and strengthen combined capabilities to compete strategically and counter common threats around the world. We seek to answer the following questions:

- What SC activities should the Army prioritize with highly capable allies?
- How have these priorities been addressed in recent contexts?
- What challenges and opportunities exist to enhance cooperation with allies?
- What mechanisms might the Army use to systematize these enhancements?

---

[1] We define *highly capable allies* as treaty allies with long histories of pursuing common objectives in coalitions; with advanced capabilities that match, complement, and/or interoperate with those of the U.S. military; and with interests in and systematic engagement portfolios with multiple countries. Such allies include Australia, Canada, France, Germany, Japan, the Republic of Korea, and the United Kingdom.

To answer these questions, we adopted a mixed-method approach that combined a literature review of findings on SC uses and effectiveness; a database analysis of recent U.S. SC; a historical analysis of secondary sources documenting recent overseas contingency operations; and interviews with key stakeholders in the United States, Australia, and the United Kingdom. Our objective was to identify insights into SC with highly capable allies from two different, but complementary, sources—lessons learned from recent overseas contingency operations and the views of our allies themselves.

As an initial step, we considered the diversity of SC activities and objectives that the United States conducts with its highly capable allies. Instead of examining SC by its traditional categorizations (i.e., authorities, mechanisms, lines of effort), we categorized SC by (1) its recipients and (2) whether the SC was meant to improve current operations or to create preconditions that would shape future operations.

We framed Army SC relationships with its highly capable allies along two dimensions. First, we examined SC with highly capable allies in terms of efforts to prepare for and synchronize military operations in coalitions (*operational partnering*) and efforts to plan, coordinate, and implement combined security engagement opportunities in third countries to support common interests (*engagement partnering*). Second, we examined SC with highly capable allies in terms of efforts to prepare partners for contemporaneous operations (*current context*) and efforts to prepare for longer-term competition (*future shaping*). We developed an analytic framework that captures the four aspects of the research in a 2x2 structure. We found this framework helpful for conducting this study and in our conversations with SC stakeholders, but further work is necessary to make it usable as a decisionmaking tool.

We found that decades of habitual U.S. relationships and activities (e.g., personnel exchanges, training, exercises) with allies have created a strong foundation for operating together in coalitions. However, even with this foundation, U.S., British, and Australian experiences in Afghanistan and Iraq suggest that these efforts are not without challenges. More-systematic mechanisms for combined contingency planning, predeployment training, incorporation of lessons learned into exercises, and tighter links between major army-to-army capstone events could improve multinational operations. More-cooperative development of concepts and systems could also enhance interoperability by systematically identifying opportunities for collaboration and for release of classified information to the closest U.S. allies.

In addition, our research indicates that multiple opportunities exist for combined planning, coordination, and implementation of SC efforts in third countries. These opportunities could serve the United States and its allies in more effectively and efficiently countering Russian and Chinese influence and enhance capabilities against other threats. Such planning and coordination among highly capable allies with presence and interests in Europe, Africa, the Middle East, and the Indo-Pacific could use the advantages of allies' strengths in particular countries and regions, creating force-multiplier effects. These effects could include greater combined access and influence in competition with common adversaries, enhanced institutional capacity building in partner nations, use of each other's political and historical strengths to reap common benefits, and more-efficient engagement through deconfliction and coordination of activities and approaches. A focused review of SC first principles with allies such as the United Kingdom, Australia, and Canada—followed by pilot initiatives with one or two allies to plan, coordinate, and implement targeted SC efforts in one or two regions—would demonstrate the utility of such cooperation and help ameliorate the challenges that occur when national interests and approaches diverge. Finally, this type of cooperation should be institutionalized in Army SC strategy and implementation plans—an effort that was in process at the time of writing—to ensure that such activities have a high profile and set the Army on a course to meet the requirements of the Army Campaign Plan and the National Defense Strategy.

Recommendations for Setting Army Security Cooperation Priorities in Operational and Engagement Partnering

The first six recommendations are derived from the findings and implications of our study of SC for operational partnering in recent and prospective operations. The second four are derived from findings and implications related to SC engagement partnering.

Priorities for Operational Partnering

1. **Establish a standing U.S.-allied land-force cell to conceptualize, exercise, and execute contingency planning for lesser state and nonstate threats.** The United States and its highly capable allies conduct deliberate planning to deter and counter near-peer threats in Europe and Asia. However, our survey of operations in Iraq and Afghanistan over the past ten to 15 years suggests that the allies did not conduct deliberate contingency or campaign planning for these operations. The absence of joint campaign planning in Iraq and Afghanistan led to misunderstandings over missions, objectives, operational strategy, the implications of national caveats, and desired end states. We suggest establishing a campaign planning cell manned by planners from the United States and its highly capable allies that focuses on lesser state and nonstate threats in regions where allies have strong interests in common with the United States. Organizational structures could already exist for creating this cell, although its creation could be a significant challenge because of potential disagreement over which contingency plans to develop, which capabilities to share, and what sacrifices each member is willing to take to execute courses of action. However, the development of frameworks, processes, and habitual planning relationships themselves would be very useful. Such contingency planning could also help identify gaps or challenges in execution that could be translated into SC requirements that partners or allies could help address.

2. **Consider more formal mechanisms for predeployment training for future contingencies against second- and third-tier threats.** Little time was devoted to joint training between the United States and its highly capable allies during operations in Iraq and Afghanistan, and we expect that this will hold true for many future operations. The United States and its highly capable allies were able to develop workarounds for building interoperability in the field; however, these require devoting limited time and resources to such development. We recommend that the Army consider engaging highly capable allies in developing concepts for jointly and rapidly spinning up forces rapidly before deployment in ways that account for the spe-

cific operational environments and missions associated with a contingency. For initial phases of pop-up contingencies (conflicts that provide little or no preparation time), coalition allies would need to rely on previous exercise and operational experiences together; this would be most feasible for longer-term combined operations and for later phases of pop-up contingencies.

3. **Identify and incorporate lessons regarding operational partnering and workarounds into exercise planning with highly capable allies.** In addition to the need for units to organically develop workarounds to ensure smooth coalition operations, there is very little evidence of follow-on efforts to maintain and internalize these interoperability gains for future contingencies. We recommend that lessons learned from Iraq and Afghanistan be identified and prioritized for incorporation into U.S.-allied exercises. The Army is already making inroads in this area through concepts associated with the Mission Partner Environment. We have identified workarounds and innovations developed jointly by the United States and its allies to mitigate challenges.

4. **Seek review of classification requirements to enable more inclusive planning and concept and system development with select allies.** Restricted releasability of classified information to allies is a perennial issue. We recommend that the Army, along with the Office of the Secretary of Defense and the Joint Staff, initiate a review of classification requirements regarding information shared with close allies (partners such as Australia, Canada, and the United Kingdom). The goal would be to enable more-inclusive planning and concept and system development with select allies. A first step would be to enumerate opportunities to forge new concepts that have been missed because of classification constraints.

5. **Identify and evaluate additional codevelopment opportunities with selected allies.** Developing a strategy for ensuring interoperability and capability modernization is a key challenge facing the Army. We recommend that the Army identify and evaluate codevelopment opportunities in both the operational and materiel spaces, where selected highly capable allies can participate as full partners in the formulation of multidomain concepts to counter future oper-

ational challenges and to jointly pursue innovative initiatives in science and technology and development of system concepts. Some work on identifying codevelopment opportunities is already underway with the United Kingdom and could be applied to other allies as well.

6. **Systematically link General Officer Roundtables (GORTs) to army-to-army staff talks.** The GORTs provide a valuable opportunity for shaping army-to-army relationships with key allies. We recommend that the Army review the goals of these meetings and their integration mechanisms with the aim of strengthening the links between them and making them more consistent. This would enhance planning for efforts aimed at operational partnering, including interoperability, and also would help set direction for engagement partnering.

Priorities for Engagement Partnering

1. **Engage highly capable allies systematically on SC first principles.** The United States and its allies lack a complete understanding of the character and complexity of each other's SC enterprises. They would benefit greatly from a dedicated effort to share first principles of SC with each other. These principles would include similarities and differences in each country's SC approaches, perceived strengths and weaknesses, and policy and legal imperatives. The geographic combatant commands and Army service component commands conduct such activities with allies in their areas of responsibility, but the interactions are relatively superficial. The Army, with the strong involvement of the relevant Army service component commands, should make a more systematic effort to understand the SC approaches of key U.S. allies with third countries and help these allies understand U.S. approaches—including each other's authorities, processes, limitations, and planning and resourcing. It is not enough to presume that U.S. allies will be willing to fall in line on U.S. SC approaches. There is a need to find common objectives and complementary ways of engaging partner countries.

2. **Develop global SC engagement plans with globally engaged highly capable allies.** The Army service component commands are primary U.S. participants in planning SC activities because of the centrality of the geographic combatant commands in defining and synchronizing SC goals and activities in their theaters. As a service and SC provider, the Army has an important role in planning SC with allied armies and other external organizations in coordination with those Army service component commands. Given that highly capable allies have interests in multiple theaters, Headquarters, Department of the Army (HQDA) should serve as an integrator that would not only provide a global, U.S. Department of Defense (DoD)–wide view of SC resource allocation but also a longer-term, service-level view of global land-power requirements while supporting theater campaign plans. Such planning efforts should be systematically implemented at the strategic level (to implement Army SC roles at the nexus of the DoD global plan and theater campaign plans) and at the operational level (for Army Service Component Command execution of theater campaign plans in regions).

3. **Conduct a pilot initiative to systematically plan, coordinate, and execute third-country engagements with one or two highly capable allies.** Building upon current U.S.-allied efforts to pursue engagements together in particular third countries (e.g., in Nigeria), as well as the initiative to improve understanding of first principles recommended earlier, we recommend that the Army consider conducting a pilot initiative with one or two Army service component commands and highly capable allies to conduct systematic combined SC planning, coordination, and execution in regions and countries of mutual priority. The effort would serve to identify areas where there is overlap and where there are gaps, where joint engagements in third countries could occur and with what SC tools, and where the United States or allies should lead combined efforts. The result could be combined engagement plans for countries and regions. These plans would integrate geographic combatant command and army service component command country plans with those of the ally.

4. **Provide guidance on SC for engagement partnering in the Army SC strategy and implementation plan.** Both documents, under development at the time of writing, should explicitly call out, institutionalize, and operationalize SC for engagement partnering with highly capable allies. Engagement partnering should be established as a priority that may bolster the U.S. and Army position in strategic competition with near-peer adversaries and in posture. The implementation plan should frame how SC for engagement partnering could be applied with allies for institutional and operational capacity building in third countries.

Conclusions

The Army's approach to working with its highly capable allies is evolving as a result of changes in national strategy and defense priorities, new DoD policies and processes, and an Army need and desire to forge a more holistic and systematic approach to its allies and partners.

Since research for this report was completed, the coronavirus disease 2019 pandemic has halted most bilateral and multilateral activities, including with Australia and the United Kingdom. The United States can no longer engage with its highly capable allies in many traditional ways, but it still needs to maintain contact and operational readiness. It is likely that the United States and the Army will need to adjust to these challenges and look for new opportunities to strengthen SC with key allies and partners. However, the crisis could provide a unique opportunity to rethink how to work with key allies to engage them and third countries.

Contents

Figure and Tables

Figure

Tables

CHAPTER ONE

Introduction

A shift in the U.S. strategic security environment has been underway during the past decade: The regional focus on countering violent extremist organizations has given way to a long-term global competition against near-peer adversaries Russia and China. The 2018 *National Defense Strategy* acknowledges an erosion of U.S. military advantage and challenges to the post–World War II international order and emphasizes "expanding competitive space" against these competitors by "strengthening alliances and attracting new partners."[1] This is a reprioritization of efforts that brings security cooperation (SC) with U.S. allies and partners to the fore.

A key part of this reprioritization is working more effectively with our closest, most-capable (*highly capable*) allies to pursue an extensive array of overlapping national interests. These highly capable allies also perceive growing threats from and competition with Russia and China while remaining concerned about transnational terrorist groups. These allies' national security strategies depend upon forging common global and regional approaches to warfighting with the United States; they also depend upon building and strengthening Western-leaning partnerships in areas of strategic import. By sharing the burden of protecting common interests, the United States and its allies can help each other achieve objectives that would be immensely challenging or impossible to achieve unilaterally. The United States and its allies recognize that in a time of increasing requirements and limited resources, they need to work together in coalitions and in engaging regional stakeholders by bringing different, valuable strengths and perspec-

---

[1] Jim Mattis, *Summary of the 2018 National Defense Strategy of the United States: Sharpening the American Military's Competitive Edge*, Washington, D.C.: U.S. Department of Defense, 2018.

tives to the combined efforts. However, although the United States and its allies recognize the importance of working together, recent operations suggest that more could be done to create and sustain mechanisms that increase the effectiveness of future joint activities.

Purpose and Key Findings

As the environment in which the United States pursues SC quickly becomes more complex and challenging, the Army seeks ways to more effectively work with its allied counterparts. In this report, we examine ways to better enable the Army to prioritize and coordinate its SC activities, in collaboration with those activities pursued by its allies and partners, to meet its assigned objectives and strengthen combined capabilities to compete strategically and counter common threats around the world. We seek to answer the following questions:

- What SC activities should the Army prioritize with highly capable allies?
- How have these priorities been addressed in recent contexts?
- What challenges and opportunities exist to enhance cooperation with allies?
- What mechanisms might the Army employ to systematize these enhancements?

Our research, completed in March 2020, focuses on the highly capable allies of the United States. We define highly capable allies as treaty allies with long histories of pursuing common objectives in coalitions; with advanced capabilities that match, complement, and/or interoperate with those of the U.S. military; and with interests in and systematic engagement portfolios with multiple countries. Such allies include Australia, Canada, France, Germany, Japan, the Republic of Korea, and the United Kingdom.

We used two main scoping criteria for our analysis. Throughout the report, we focus on the United Kingdom and Australia rather than the broader set of U.S. highly capable allies. We do so for three reasons. First, the Army has a long tradition of working closely and intensively with both nations. Current and past SC activities and operations among the United States, the United Kingdom, and Australia provide a wealth of experience from which to consider best practices for prioritizing future SC. Second, the Army has been working with its counterparts in the United Kingdom and Australia to further institutionalize SC, as we discuss in greater detail in Chapter Five. Therefore, findings for improving SC prioritization between the United States, the United Kingdom, and Australia can immediately better Army efforts. Third, senior army and defense officials in the United Kingdom and Australia provided support and access to the study team. This increased our ability to identify and validate findings across all three countries. Experiences with and lessons from engagement with other allies (such as Canada, France, and Germany) differ somewhat from those with the United Kingdom and Australia; we highlight these differences throughout the report.

Although we provide a broad overview of recent U.S., British, and Australian SC and U.S., British, and Australian perspectives about opportunities and challenges for collaboration, we focus on recent overseas contingency operations in Iraq, Syria, and Afghanistan. We do so for two reasons. First, these were recent, large, multiyear, coalition operations that included a wide variety of warfighting functions for all three countries. They capture the complexity, if not the near-peer characteristics, of future scenarios of interest to the Army. Second, this study grew out of a request to identify lessons learned for prioritizing SC with highly capable allies based on SC undertaken in preparation for and during operations in Iraq, Syria, and Afghanistan. We extract broader findings and recommendations for U.S. and Army SC strategy for and planning with highly capable allies. We expect that these findings will have valuable insights for the Army as it prepares for potential competition and conflict with potential near-peer adversaries and lesser contingencies.

We frame Army SC relationships with its highly capable allies in terms of efforts to prepare for and synchronize military operations in coalitions (*operational partnering*) and efforts to plan, coordinate, and implement combined security engagement opportunities in *third countries* (countries in which the United States and its allies jointly conduct SC) to support common interests (*engagement partnering*). These concepts are further defined in Chapter Two. Our findings suggest that decades of habitual U.S. relationships and activities (e.g., personnel exchanges, training, exercises) with these allies have laid important foundations for effectively operating together in coalitions, but Afghanistan and Iraq demonstrated that these efforts are not without challenges. Such challenges could be mitigated with more systematic mechanisms for combined contingency planning, predeployment training, incorporation of lessons learned into exercises, and tighter links between major army-to-army capstone events. More-cooperative development of concepts and systems could result in enhanced interoperability through efforts to systematically identify opportunities for collaboration and to review releasability of classified information to the closest U.S. allies.

In addition, our research indicates that multiple opportunities exist for combined planning, coordination, and implementation of SC efforts in third countries. These opportunities could serve the United States and its allies in more effectively and efficiently countering Russian and Chinese influence and in enhancing capabilities against other threats. Such planning and coordination among highly capable allies with presence and interests in Europe, Africa, the Middle East, and the Indo-Pacific could have a force-multiplier effect—including a better-coordinated effort to compete globally with near-peer adversaries—and take advantage of each ally's strengths in particular countries and regions. Our findings suggest that a focused review of SC first principles with such allies as the United Kingdom, Australia, and Canada—followed by a pilot initiative with one or two allies to plan, coordinate, and implement targeted SC efforts in one or two regions—would demonstrate the utility of such U.S.-allied cooperation. Finally, this type of cooperation should be institutionalized in Army SC strategy and implementation plans to ensure that such activities have a high profile and set the Army on a course to meet the requirements of the Army Campaign Plan and the National Defense Strategy.

Framing Security Cooperation with Highly Capable Allies

The U.S. Congress defines SC as

> any program, activity (including an exercise), or interaction of the Department of Defense with the security establishment of a foreign

country to achieve a purpose as follows: (A) to build and develop allied and friendly security capabilities for self-defense and multinational operations; (B) to provide the armed forces with access to the foreign country in peacetime or a contingency operation; (C) to promote relationships that promote specific United States security interests.[2]

The *Department of Defense Dictionary of Military and Associated Terms* reflects this congressional definition, stating that SC is

all Department of Defense interactions with foreign security establishments to build security relationships that promote specific United States security interests, develop allied and partner nation military and security capabilities for self-defense and multinational operations, and provide United States forces with peacetime and contingency access to allied and partner nations.[3]

The joint publication also states that security assistance—efforts governed by the Foreign Assistance Act of 1961 and the Arms Export Control Act of 1976 to provide defense articles, military training, and other defense-related services by grant, loan, credit, or cash—is an SC element.

SC with highly capable allies has become an important component of U.S. defense strategy. According to the *National Defense Strategy*, deepening strategic planning and interoperability with allies and partners is critical to enabling U.S. forces to operate successfully in a future security environment.[4] The United States' closest allies have also made it a priority to engage with the U.S. military to improve their ability to face common security threats. SC is a U.S. term, and U.S. allies often use different terms for SC, such as *defense engagement* in the United Kingdom or *international engage-*

[2] Public Law 114-328, National Defense Authorization Act for Fiscal Year 2017, January 4, 2016, pp. 499–500.

[3] Joint Publication 1-02, *DoD Dictionary of Military and Associated Terms*, Washington, D.C.: Joint Chiefs of Staff, November 2019, pp. 191–192. See also Joint Publication 3-20, *Security Cooperation*, Washington, D.C.: Joint Chiefs of Staff, May 23, 2017, p. 5, and Department of Defense Directive 5132.03, *DoD Policy and Responsibilities Relating to Security Cooperation*, Washington, D.C.: Office of the Under Secretary of Defense for Policy, December 29, 2016, p. 17.

[4] Mattis, 2018.

ment in Australia. However, all these terms express the idea that cooperation with foreign partner security forces and institutions is intended to advance mutual security interests.

SC activities include military-to-military contacts, workshops and conferences, individual and unit training, professional military education, exercises, development and provision of military equipment, planning and subject-matter expert exchanges, key leader engagements, and other U.S.-partner interactions. Given the advanced status of capabilities of and U.S. relationships with highly capable allies, U.S. SC with them is expansive, focusing on enhancing interoperability, improving combined concepts of operation and approaches to security challenges, and maintaining enduring, close security relationships. The United States and its allies conduct sophisticated exercises, codevelop, and acquire major items of military equipment, collaborate closely in science and technology innovations, embed personnel in each other's defense institutions (often at very senior levels), and hold frequent leadership and staff talks to work on issues together.[5]

SC with highly capable allies and other partners is often described as a means of sharing the burden of worldwide security requirements. However, the term *burden-sharing* has negative connotations; allies can interpret it as the United States seeking to offload a burden onto them.[6] Therefore, we do not use the term in this report.

We focus on two important outputs to SC with highly capable allies. The first output is the ability to operate together in coalition operations against common threats because the United States and its allies have the same or compatible objectives, concepts of operation, military equipment and systems, and tactics, techniques, and procedures (TTPs)—or because they complement each other with niche capabilities that fill gaps in or improve

---

[5] We note that some events, such as multilateral exercises to improve interoperability, might fit the SC definition but have other important objectives, such as enhancing the operational readiness of U.S. forces. For the purposes of this report, we highlight the SC elements of these events and do not distinguish readiness-related objectives.

[6] The National Defense Strategy clearly reflects the negative connotation of the term, stating that "when we pool resources and share responsibility for our common defense, our security burden becomes lighter" (Mattis, 2018, p. 8).

coalition capabilities. We call this *SC for operational partnering*.[7] SC for operational partnering with highly capable allies includes planning conferences to prepare for combined execution of coalition operations and codevelopment of (and mutual investment in) capabilities designed to improve interoperability. Some constraints to operational partnering include national caveats restricting the use of a partner's military assets, disparities in capabilities, and restrictive national policies on information sharing. SC professionals should strive to reduce the impact of these constraints.

The second output is the ability to build the military and institutional capacity of third countries and gain influence in and access to those partners in a coordinated, synchronized way to achieve common country-specific, regional, and global objectives. These objectives include jointly countering Russian and Chinese influence.[8] We call this *SC for engagement partnering*. Ideally, such SC would increase the combined effect of Western engagement with third countries by encouraging each ally to focus on areas of competitive advantage (e.g., where there is third-country sensitivity to working with the United States or one of its allies). This effect could include greater combined access and influence in competition with common adversaries, enhanced institutional capacity building in partner nations, use of each other's political and historical strengths to reap common benefits, and more-efficient engagement through deconfliction and coordination of activities and approaches. In some cases, one ally could take a lead role in a third country while conducting extensive behind-the-scenes information-sharing and coordination with the others at the appropriate levels. SC for engagement partnering with highly capable allies might include staff talks to establish common objectives, new planning practices that enable smooth division of labor in U.S.-allied engagement with third countries, and definitions of common training methods.

---

[7]   See Christopher G. Pernin, Angela O'Mahony, Gene Germanovich, and Matthew Lane, *Chasing Multinational Interoperability: Benefits, Objectives, and Strategies*, Santa Monica, Calif.: RAND Corporation, RR-3068-A, 2020.

[8]   There are certainly other important outputs to SC with highly capable allies. For example, the United States might wish to help empower a highly capable partner to take on security challenges alone (not in coalition) by providing weapons systems and sharing operational concepts. In other cases, access might remain an important SC goal.

Constraints can make engagement partnering challenging, especially at the strategic level. These challenges include misaligned priorities and self-interest, the capacity of third countries to absorb U.S. or allied assistance, different standard operating procedures, and even competition for military sales among allies. Again, it is incumbent upon SC professionals to recognize and mitigate these constraints. Executing operational and engagement partnering effectively requires careful preparation, coordination, practice, and, above all, planning—the heart of U.S. SC with highly capable allies that is currently less systematic and coordinated than is desirable.

Methodology and Organization of Report

Throughout this study, we focus on addressing the research questions in the context of both operational partnering and engagement partnering with highly capable allies. To answer these questions, we adopted a mixed-method approach (summarized in the appendix) that combined a literature review of previous findings on SC uses and effectiveness, a database analysis of recent U.S. SC, a historical analysis of secondary sources documenting recent overseas contingency operations, and interviews with key stakeholders in the United States, the United Kingdom, and Australia. Our objective with this approach was to identify SC insights for operational and engagement partnering from two different but complementary directions—recent overseas contingency operations and shaping capabilities with the allies themselves.

First, we explored U.S.-allied SC in the context of overseas contingency operations in Afghanistan (Operation Enduring Freedom [OEF] and Resolute Support Mission [RSM]) and in Iraq and Syria (Operation Iraqi Freedom [OIF] and Operation Inherent Resolve [OIR]) to assess how lessons learned from these operations could be brought forward into U.S. planning and coordination with allies. We sought to understand how the United States and its allies collaborated on the planning and execution of operations and of efforts to train local security forces. SC activities conducted with allies in the context of Iraq and Afghanistan were different from other SC activities that the Army conducts from the standpoint of scope, authority, resourcing, and partner dynamics; however, we sought to extract lessons that are applicable to other types of contingency operations and SC initiatives. For this part of the research we relied on a review of secondary sources, including detailed histories such as the British Chilcot Report and interviews with current and former British and Australian commanders who had deployed to these operations. We also undertook a broad overview of U.S. SC activities, as captured in the Department of Defense's (DoD's) Global Theater SC Management Information System (G-TSCMIS), to identify representative uses of SC with highly capable allies.[9]

Second, we sought to identify challenges and opportunities for future U.S.-allied collaboration based on lessons learned from OEF/RSM and OIR/OIF and on the perspectives of two highly capable allies, the United Kingdom and Australia, which have been among the most capable and consistent partners in these operations. We focused on interviews with key stakeholders in those two countries at the strategic and operational levels. We elicited allied perspectives on future coalition overseas contingency operations and on joint engagement in regions of common interest to help prioritize SC objectives and mechanisms of interest to both the United States and its allies. This included subject matter experts in embassies in Washington, defense and foreign affairs ministries and departments, SC organizations, planning staffs, and unit commanders. A list of organizations with whom we engaged and an interview protocol developed for this purpose can be found in the appendix.

We received detailed comments for each interview (interviewees were assured that interview responses would be anonymized). Almost all interviews lasted at least an hour. Across our interviews, we found broad agreement in terms of when SC was present or absent and why SC occurred. We encountered greater variation in interviewees' reflections on how to address potential shortcomings in SC with highly capable allies.

Our research approach was exploratory, rather than confirmatory. We drew on each of the research methods described above, as well as our SC subject-matter expertise, to identify lessons and develop recommendations for the Army to consider for planning SC with highly capable allies. Our

---

[9] G-TSCMIS was scheduled to be replaced by a new management system, known as Socium, in December 2020.

approach to this report is to present our research concisely in the context of easily digestible findings, implications, and recommendations.

As we were conducting the research for this report, the sponsor asked us to support the Army in drafting a SC strategy and plan to institutionalize and operationalize SC throughout the Army enterprise in support of the DoD guidance, laws and regulations, and the *Army Campaign Plan 2019+*. We directly supported the Headquarters, Department of the Army (HQDA) initiative to develop a SC implementation plan that would provide coherent, holistic direction to the Army on allies and partners. At the time of writing, this initiative was ongoing. The simultaneity of the two efforts enabled us to inform the draft implementation plan and foster an understanding of Army SC mechanisms that could be incorporated into this report.

Chapter Two describes the conceptual framework in more detail and provides examples of U.S. SC with its highly capable allies in each of the framework's component parts. Chapters Three and Four apply the conceptual framework and describe findings and implications derived from our exploration of operational partnering and engagement partnering, respectively. Finally, in Chapter Five, we examine the Army's effort to develop a SC strategy and implementation plan and offer recommendations based on our operational and engagement partnering research. The appendix provides our research approach.

After we completed the research for this report, the coronavirus disease 2019 (COVID-19) pandemic struck, leading to the postponement or cancellation of numerous SC activities—including with the United States' closest allies. We provide some preliminary thoughts in Chapter Five on potential effects of the pandemic on near- and farther-term SC with highly capable allies.

CHAPTER TWO

An Analytic Framework for Security Cooperation with Highly Capable Allies

We focus on two primary objectives of U.S. SC engagement with its key allies: (1) to strengthen U.S. and highly capable allies' capabilities to execute operations together (SC to enable operational partnering) and (2) to enable third parties to develop, maintain, and use capabilities to undertake operations in keeping with U.S. and allied priorities, preferences, and objectives (SC to enable engagement partnering with allies). This chapter presents an analytic framework for understanding the different ways in which the United States works with its highly capable allies to achieve these objectives for both current and future operations.

SC encompasses a variety of activities that are meant to achieve a diverse set of objectives, such as building relationships that promote U.S. security interests, developing partners' capabilities for self-defense and multinational operations, and securing access for U.S. forces. The 2019 *Defense Institute for Security Cooperation Studies Handbook* lists over 100 active SC programs, which generate thousands of engagements with U.S. allies and partners each year.[1] These activities are carried out across the DoD and allies' ministries and departments of defense and military services. It is important to remember that none of these organizations are unitary actors. All are bureaucratic organizations in which individual offices and units have different priorities and responsibilities for engaging with allies and partners.

---

[1] Defense Security Cooperation University, *Security Cooperation Programs Handbook*, Washington, D.C., 2021.

Within the Army, the activities and objectives included under the umbrella of SC are undertaken by different parts of the force. For example, exercises to increase interoperability can be carried out by the G-3 or the component commands, and training partner units at the tactical level might fall under the purview of a Security Force Assistance Brigade. Army personnel may also be involved in SC engagements through the combatant commands, by participating in multinational forces, or by serving as liaisons in joint or allied headquarter commands.

This diversity of activity and actors is even more apparent among U.S. allies. The British Ministry of Defense has prioritized engagement activities with the United States and strives to be the U.S. partner of choice.[2] The British Army conducts SC with other partners as well. Britain's Regionally Aligned Brigades are involved in persistent capacity-building activities and its Specialised Infantry Group provides episodic training for niche signals and cyber capabilities. As of January 2019, the Specialised Infantry Group had forces deployed in Iraq, Afghanistan, Nigeria, Cameroon, Kenya, and Djibouti.[3] Unlike the United Kingdom, the Australian Army has no specialized forces dedicated to SC. Instead, it aligns battalions with a particular partner of interest. These partners of interest include Papua New Guinea, Fiji, and Tonga.[4] As with the United Kingdom, Australia also prioritizes opportunities to work with the Army, especially in the Indo-Pacific region.

The United States, the United Kingdom, and Australia organize for and conceptualize SC differently; they each use SC as an important mechanism to meet their national security objectives. Therefore, we adopt an objectives-based framework in this study to best capture the entirety of SC and to enable SC prioritization. We categorize activities by their purpose—either

---

[2] The United Kingdom has focused on improving interoperability with the United States through exercises, codevelopment initiatives, and opportunities to collaborate more closely with the United States in the science and technology sector.

[3] Specialised Infantry Group briefing, January 22, 2019. Not available to the general public. The largest Specialised Infantry Group deployment was 33 personnel in Afghanistan and the average deployment per country is roughly 20 personnel, according to the briefing.

[4] Dwayne M. Butler, Angelena Bohman, Lisa Pelled Colabella, Julia A. Thompson, Michael Shurkin, Stephan B. Seabrook, Rebecca Jensen, and Christina Bartol Burnett, *Comprehensive Analysis of Strategic Force Generation Challenges in the Australian Army*, Santa Monica, Calif.: RAND Corporation, RR-2382-AUS, 2018.

to improve the ability of the United States and its allies to operate together in current or future operations or to improve their ability to operate with or build the capacity of third countries now or in the future. This objective-centered approach is intended to place SC discussions in a strategic context and to set the stage for future discussions on how SC activities could be better prioritized and scoped to meet common military objectives.

Analytic Approach to Security Cooperation with Highly Capable Allies

As an initial step, we considered the diversity of SC activities and objectives that the United States conducts with its highly capable allies. We reviewed joint and Army guidance documents on SC—such as Joint Publication 3-20, *Security Cooperation*, and Army Pamphlet 11-31, *Army Security Coopera-tion Handbook*—as well as past RAND works, which list SC activities across the spectrum of partners.

In light of our interest in SC with highly capable allies, we stepped back from the traditional categorizations of SC (by authorities, activities, mecha-nisms, and lines of effort). Instead, we focused on who was receiving the SC and whether the SC was aimed at improving current operations and set-ting preconditions to shape future operations. This approach let us look for broader patterns that would be useful for identifying recommendations for prioritizing SC with highly capable allies.

Overall, we found this framework helpful for conducting this study and for our interviews with SC stakeholders, and we believe that our approach matches practitioners' intuition. That said, we emphasize at the outset that, because the framework is not currently aligned with SC planning, resourc-ing, and implementation, further work is necessary to operationalize it as an Army decisionmaking tool.

Table 2.1 summarizes the analytic framework that we use in our approach to understanding U.S. SC with highly capable allies.

The rows of the framework capture the two overarching objectives for conducting SC with highly capable allies that are the focus of our research—to improve operational partnering and to coordinate combined engage-ment with third-country partners. The columns capture whether the SC

TABLE 2.1

Analytic Framework for Security Cooperation with Highly Capable Allies

Type of Partnering	Current Operations	Future Shaping
SC for operational partnering (enabling coalition operations with highly capable allies)	• Improve capabilities for current operation • Share information for current operation • Develop workarounds	• Improve interoperability for future operations • Establish shared standards and procedures • Aid codevelopment of capabilities
SC for engagement partnering (coordinating with highly capable allies for SC in third countries)	• Build local security force military capacity • Improve capabilities for third parties to contribute to current coalition operations	• Build partner capacity for future operations • Gain access and influence • Improve strategic competitiveness

focused on executing contemporaneous or *current operations* (such as SC that occurred concurrently with operations in Iraq and Afghanistan) or on preparing for long-term competition (*future shaping*).

Within each of the table cells, we list common tasks for each type of SC based on U.S. SC in recent years. It is important to note that, although we list tasks that are archetypical for each cell, they are not exclusive to one cell. For example, procedures for deconfliction and interoperability to improve current operations will have similarities with improving interoperability for future shaping. This framework builds on findings from previous RAND SC research and discussions with U.S. and allied practitioners on what activities are undertaken when and for what purposes.[5]

---

[5]   See Angela O'Mahony, Thomas S. Szayna, Christopher G. Pernin, Laurinda L. Rohn, Derek Eaton, Elizabeth Bodine-Baron, Joshua Mendelsohn, Osonde A. Osoba, Sherry Oehler, Katharina Ley Best, and Leila Bighash, *The Global Landpower Network: Recommendations for Strengthening Army Engagement*, Santa Monica, Calif.: RAND Corporation, RR-1813-A, 2017; Jefferson P. Marquis, Michael J. McNerney, S. Rebecca Zimmerman, Merrie Archer, Jeremy Boback, and David Stebbins, *Developing an Assessment, Monitoring, and Evaluation Framework for U.S. Department of Defense Security Cooperation*, Santa Monica, Calif.: RAND Corporation, RR-1611-OSD, 2016; and Jennifer D. P. Moroney, Celeste Gventer, Stephanie Pezard, and Laurence Smallman, *Lessons from U.S. Allies in Security Cooperation with Third Countries: The Cases of Australia, France, and the United Kingdom*, Santa Monica, Calif.: RAND Corporation, TR-972-AF, 2011.

Examples of Security Cooperation with Highly Capable Allies: Operational Partnering

We discuss each type of SC in detail in the following sections. We begin by examining the broad category of SC activities that focus on enabling coalition operations. These are the most common types of engagements undertaken with highly capable allies; they apply to both current and future operations. In Table 2.2, we provide illustrative examples.

Operational Partnering in Current Operations

SC engagement for current operations includes activities that are more immediate in nature and are focused on preparing allied or coalition forces to operate jointly in ongoing combat. These activities tend to focus on ensuring that each respective force has a common understanding of each other's bilateral or multilateral objectives and that they have comparable concepts of operations. To better illustrate these activities, we describe them based on the following three objectives that SC was designed to accomplish during recent operations:

1. improving capabilities relevant to the current operation
2. sharing information based on recent and ongoing experiences in theater

TABLE 2.2

Examples of Security Cooperation with Highly Capable Allies for Operational Partnering

Type of Security Cooperation	Current Operations	Future Shaping
SC for operational partnering (enabling coalition operations with highly capable allies)	• U.S.-German Medical Evacuation training prior to ISAF mission Afghanistan • NATO Joint Analysis and Lessons Learned Centre • Special Forces coordination cell for OIR	• Warfighter Exercise and Joint Warfighting Assessment • Talisman Sabre/Defender exercises • U.S.-Republic of Korea Capabilities and Research Cooperation Cooperative • Research Testing Development and Evaluation programs

NOTE: ISAF = International Security Assistance Force; NATO = North Atlantic Treaty Organization.

3. working out procedures for deconfliction and improving interoperability in the current operation (i.e., workarounds).

Although these objectives were typical of SC during current operations, they are not exclusive to current operations. Unlike SC in long-term competition, SC in current operations is more likely to emerge in response to operational needs rather than through the multiyear planning process that typifies SC in steady state.[6]

Improving Current Operationally Relevant Capabilities

In an ideal world, SC in competition provides sufficient opportunities to develop effective interoperability between highly capable allies prior to coalition operations. However, experience in recent operations has shown that steady state training for the "fight tonight" has not always been sufficient. As a result, there is a role for SC activities—either immediately prior to an operation or early on during an operation—to improve allies' operationally relevant capabilities.

One way that U.S. and allied forces can prepare to operate together is to train or exercise together before deploying. Although there is often less time to exercise prior to current operations, even short-term engagements might help ensure more-compatible TTPs and improve interoperability. We identified a variety of U.S. predeployment SC activities to exercise joint capabilities through our analysis of activities included in G-TSCMIS and present a few of them here. Before engaging in ISAF missions in Afghanistan, U.S. and German forces undertook predeployment medical evacuation training to enable greater coordination in the field.[7] Similarly, U.S. and Canadian forces engaged in joint personnel recovery training. NATO forces rotating into ISAF participated in Exercise Unified Endeavor, which provided simulated training designed to improve decisionmaking among the twenty

---

[6] SC planners at U.S. Army Europe have discussed the "operationalization of SC" that occurs during operations, which is not planned or accounted for in the same way as steady state SC (O'Mahony et al., 2017, p. 97).

[7] See the appendix for details on the G-TSCMIS analysis that we conducted for this research. G-TSCMIS data are not available to the general public.

national forces on the ground in Afghanistan.[8] Other predeployment training has taken place with multiple partners engaged in operations in Afghanistan and Iraq through NATO's Joint Force Training Centre.[9]

Sharing Information for Current Operations

Once in theater, highly capable allies have identified the need for processes to learn from one another, especially in the face of unanticipated challenges and an evolving operational environment. The sharing of information and lessons learned to facilitate operations is a form of SC that occurs regularly among the United States and its highly capable allies. For example, in Afghanistan, U.S. and NATO forces benefited from their British counterparts setting up learning sessions to share lessons and TTPs on the use of intelligence, surveillance, and reconnaissance for targeting.[10] Intelligence sharing is also a common form of SC for operational partnering, and it is often governed by more-formal agreements and by such mechanisms as memoranda of understanding or General Security of Military Information Agreements. Among Five Eye countries (Australia, Canada, New Zealand, the United Kingdom, and the United States), there are both formal intelligence-sharing agreements and less-formal mechanisms developed through longstanding relationships among intelligence organizations. These mechanisms have been developed through conducting operations in Iraq and Afghanistan and global counterterrorism operations that facilitate information sharing.[11]

Multinational forums are another means for facilitating the sharing of information for current operations. Pre-existing multinational security forums, such as the American, British, Canadian, Australian and New Zea-

---

[8] Michael Beaton, "Unified Endeavor 14-01 Prepares U.S./Multinational Soldiers for ISAF Deployment," U.S. Army, webpage, October 16, 2013.

[9] NATO Joint Force Training Centre, "Pre-Deployment Training for NATO Mission Iraq. New Task for JFTC," press release, May 16, 2019.

[10] This example is based on one interviewee's experience working in the NATO headquarters in 2018 for NATO's Resolute Support Mission.

[11] Michael E. DeVine, *United States Foreign Intelligence Relationships: Background, Policy and Legal Authorities, Risks, Benefits*, Washington, D.C.: Congressional Research Service, R45720, May 15, 2019.

land Armies Program (ABCANZ) and NATO, are often associated with information sharing during long-term competition. They also provide mechanisms to collect and disseminate lessons on current large operations. In the case of ABCANZ, lessons learned tended to be framed in terms of standards. For example, in response to an identified gap in the lead nation framework and concept used in Afghanistan, an ABCANZ meeting was devoted to developing an ABCANZ standard for coalition command and control at the tactical level. In addition, ABCANZ has hosted exercises and developed assessment metrics for operational outcomes. In 2017, NATO's Joint Intelligence and Security Division was established to track threats emanating from the hybrid domain, cyber space, and terrorism.[12] NATO's Joint Analysis and Lessons Learned Centre also performs joint analysis of operations, training, exercises and experiments and supports the exchange of lessons to the NATO training community.

Developing Workarounds

Finally, a third means of engaging with high capability allies for current operational partnering involves the exchange of information, intelligence, and development of coordination mechanisms—also known as developing workarounds. This type of engagement often evolves from interpersonal relations between allies. Face-to-face availability and exchanges are one of the most common types of SC between operational partners, as they allow real-time troubleshooting and knowledge exchange. Liaisons and exchange personnel can help with this type of SC, as in Afghanistan, where British liaison officers were deployed to NATO headquarters, or during the planning of OIR, in which a coordination cell was established at U.S. Special Operations Command headquarters to improve communication between allied special forces.[13]

---

[12] Arndt Freytag von Loringhoven, "Adapting NATO Intelligence in Support of 'One NATO,'" *NATO Review*, September 8, 2017.

[13] Lessons Learned Operations and Strategic Studies Branch, U.S. Special Operations Command, *Multinational SOF Planning Insights: Operation Inherent Resolve*, Tampa, Fla., April 23, 2015.

Operational Partnering for Future Shaping

SC between the United States and allies for future operational partnering is the most common type of SC we observed between highly capable allies and is a mainstay of long-term competition. This type of SC focuses on developing capabilities for future coalition operations. Most recently, such SC activities have focused on preparing for possible near-peer conflict. These activities are most often conducted to meet three broad objectives: (1) creating exercises to improve interoperability, (2) establishing shared standards and procedures, and (3) developing compatible military technology and weapons systems and acquiring interoperable materiel. As concern grows over the potential of a near-peer conflict, these objectives have gained increasing emphasis in defense planning and are priorities for SC with highly capable allies.

Exercising to Improve Interoperability

As the United States and its allies have become more concerned about preparing for a potential highly capable fight in either Europe or the Pacific, they have focused on demonstrating the ability of their forces to operate together. Exercising to improve interoperability is seen as critical to both deterring or succeeding in a future war and has thus become a priority for SC with key allies. This is most evident in the greater emphasis placed on large-scale bilateral and multinational exercises. Multinational versions of warfighter exercises and joint warfighting assessments are two examples of ongoing exercises that have increasingly prioritized interoperability with allies. In April 2018, 1,000 British soldiers from the 3rd Division were involved in the U.S. Warfighter Exercise at Fort Bragg; the exercise simulated a massive conflict against a near-peer threat.[14] In Joint Warfighting Assessment 2019, 6,000 joint and multinational troops engaged in an exercise that focused on improving coalition data sharing among other aspects of interoperability during operations in a major conflict.[15] U.S. Defender

---

[14] Drew Brooks, "U.S., U.K. Forces Engage in a New Kind of Training at Bragg," *Fayetteville Observer*, April 11, 2018.

[15] Bob Morrison, "US Army Joint Warfighting Assessment 19," Joint-Forces.com, webpage, May 19, 2019; Rich Marsh, "Joint Warfighting Assessment 2019: Seven Nations Meet to Finalize Plans," U.S. Army, webpage, January 25, 2019.

exercises have also shifted to focus on major conflicts in Europe and a South China Sea scenario in the Pacific.[16]

The United States engages with Australia in the biannual Talisman Sabre exercise, which is meant to improve operational effectiveness and interoperability. Talisman Sabre 2019 was designed to practice planning and conducting combined and joint task force operations to improve the combat readiness and interoperability between U.S. and Australian forces in a future conflict.[17] The United States and Australia have also been able to engage in virtual exercises through the Queensland-based Joint Combined Training Centre that links Australian and U.S. exercise headquarters to combine live training action with computer-generated simulations and platform simulators around the world.[18]

Establishing Shared Standards and Procedures

The United States and its allies prioritize establishing shared standards and procedures to ensure that they have the ability to coordinate effectively in a potential conflict. Liaisons and personnel exchanges provide a way to sustain enduring relationships between U.S. and allied militaries. The United States conducts SC activities on a bilateral basis, engaging allies in liaison and military personnel exchange programs. The United Kingdom has as many as 15 liaison officers and 13 exchange officers placed in Army commands. These officers have the opportunity to share information on operational procedures, which helps build and sustain long-term interoperability between the two armies.[19]

---

[16] Jen Judson, "US Army's 'Defender Pacific' Drill to Focus on South China Sea Scenario," *Defense News*, March 27, 2019a; Jen Judson, "Reforger Redux? Defender 2020 to Be 3rd Largest Exercise in Europe Since Cold War," Defense News, October 7, 2019b.

[17] Ashley Maldonado-Suarez, "Exercise Talisman Sabre 2019: Demonstrates High Mobility Artillery Rocket System in Australia," U.S. Indo-Pacific Command, press release, July 10, 2019.

[18] "US and Australian Troops Go Virtual," *Arms Technology*, June 29, 2007.

[19] Outside the British Army, approximately 200 British officers are on exchange across the other services; about 800 British personnel are in the United States conducting a variety of activities, from flying remotely piloted aircraft systems to cyberspace operations (author interview with senior British defense officials, 2019).

Defense and military contacts, which are more short-term, also provide a means for sharing information. The contacts include army-to-army staff talks and key leader and senior leader engagements. According to G-TSCMIS, Australia and the United Kingdom have the highest number of SC engagements among highly capable partners, including planning conferences, bilateral and multilateral coordination meetings, and staff talks; the majority of these engagements are focused on interoperability.

Multilateral engagements and such organizations as NATO and ABCANZ provide mechanisms for developing shared standards for the United States and its allies. NATO Standardization Agreements, for example, provide the basis for developing common operational and administrative procedures and logistics that enable one NATO country to operate with and support another member's military forces. ABCANZ focuses on developing common standards for the land forces of the highly capable allies. Regional working groups have also developed in recent years to serve as an institutional mechanism to share information. Together, they have become part of an emerging SC planning process initiated by the United States and its highly capable allies.

Developing Compatible Military Technology and Weapon Systems

Coordination with allies on the development of weapons technology aimed toward improving interoperability has gained greater attention in recent years. Increased U.S.-British technical interoperability was the purpose of a 2020 Memorandum of Agreement between the U.S. Secretary of the Army and the British Minister of Defence, which emphasized the development of a bilateral modernization plan that covers several modernization activities. This agreement led the Army's Futures Command to conduct a series of modernization workshops to collaborate on networks, long-range precision fires, future vertical lift, soldier lethality, and precision navigation and timing to create more interoperable systems.[20] These modernization workshops contribute to higher-level U.S.-British Capabilities and Research Cooperation–Army talks and U.S.-British General Officer Roundtables (GORTs).

---

[20] Carol Scheina, "U.S. and U.K. Armies Align Science and Technology Modernization Plans," U.S. Army, press release, September 30, 2020.

The United States has cooperative research development test and evaluation and science and technology programs with countries throughout the world, but its cooperative production arrangements are primarily with its highly capable allies. Both Australia and the United Kingdom have signed defense trade cooperation treaties with the United States to meet specific operational and cooperative requirements. These treaties allow for the exchange of technology that would otherwise be limited by export controls and afford opportunities for combined research and coordination that can improve interoperability in the long term.

The relationship with Australia is underpinned by an agreement on science and technology cooperation. The 2007 U.S.-Australia Defense Trade Treaty underpins this trade, permitting the license-free export of most defense articles between the two countries in support of combined military operations, cooperative defense research, and other projects for government end use.[21] U.S.-British defense technology exchanges are covered under the U.S. DoD–British Ministry of Defence Reciprocal Defense Procurement memorandum of understanding that was amended in January 2018.[22] These are long-standing agreements that provide the framework for defense technology exchanges.

Examples of Security Cooperation with Highly Capable Allies: Engagement Partnering

A second broad category of SC between the United States and its highly capable allies involves the coordination of efforts and focused planning to prepare other partners to participate in ongoing or future operations and to conduct SC together in third countries. The purposes of such forms of

---

[21] U.S. Embassy and Consulates in Australia, "AUSMIN 2017 Fact Sheet on the U.S.–Australia Relationship," webpage, June 5, 2017.

[22] Department of Defense of the United States of America and the Secretary of State for Defence of the United Kingdom of Great Britain and Northern Ireland, "Memorandum of Understanding Between the Department of Defense of the United States of America and the Secretary of State for Defence of the United Kingdom of Great Britain and Northern Ireland Concerning Reciprocal Defense Procurement," January 2018.

engagement are often to (1) build the military capacity of local security forces or (2) improve the ability of third parties to contribute to coalition forces. There are important benefits to the United States and its closest allies in planning and coordinating efforts in third countries. In areas in which allies have identical or similar interests and objectives—such as countries critical to competing with common adversaries—engagement partnering can allow the allies to deconflict activities and more efficiently determine the most advantageous SC focus areas for each ally to pursue based on its political, military, cultural, historical, and other strengths.

The extent to which SC activities with partners are coordinated often depends on the priorities and objectives of the United States and its allies in relation to those third countries. As we will discuss in Chapter Four, there is less coordination of SC with third countries than U.S., British or Australian planners would often prefer. We provide examples in Table 2.3.

Engagement Partnering in Current Operations

In recent years, SC with highly capable allies for engagement with third countries for current operations has focused heavily on efforts to build local national security forces in Iraq and Afghanistan and building partner capacity for coalition partners. These activities have been designed to ensure that

TABLE 2.3

Examples of Security Cooperation with Highly Capable Allies for Engagement Partnering

Type of Security Cooperation	Current Operations	Future Shaping
SC for engagement partnering (coordinating with highly capable allies for SC in third countries)	• U.S. training of Eastern European forces for ISAF mission in Afghanistan • British training of Jordanians for ISAF mission • Australian-U.S. coordination on UH-60 program in Afghanistan	• Transatlantic Capability Enhancement and Training Initiative (TACET) • Australia's Pacific Step Up to compete with Chinese influence • U.S.-British Strategic Effects and Forces Alignment Board • Multinational Coordination Center at U.S. Africa Command

the allies have a common approach for building—and a common understanding of the uses for—partner capabilities.

Building Capacity of Local Security Forces

Many U.S. military engagements over the past two decades have included a training component aimed at training local forces to either enable an intervention or facilitate a withdrawal.[23] Afghanistan provides a prime example of an effort in which both the United States and its allies have invested heavily in training local forces. The United Kingdom has been engaged in training efforts with the United States since 2003 and continues to provide mentors who work in a training and advisory role within the Afghan National Army Officers' Academy and Infantry Branch School, among other Afghan institutions. As part of the counter–Islamic State of Iraq and Syria (ISIS) effort, the United Kingdom coordinated with the United States in supporting five training bases in Iraq in late 2018. British trainers also took the lead in training Peshmerga in Erbil in counter–improvised explosive device (IED), medical, and engineering skills.[24] Similarly, Australia took the lead for a special operations task group advising and assisting the Iraqi Counter Terrorism Service during OIR. Australia and New Zealand also established an academy for training noncommissioned officers for the Iraqi Army in Taji.[25]

Improving Partner Capacity to Contribute to Current Coalition Operations

The United States and its allies have also worked both in parallel and together to train third party forces to engage in coalition operations. The United States invested in training Eastern European forces to participate in stability operations in Afghanistan with train and equip funds while the

---

[23] France engaged in similar efforts to build up the armies of Mali, Burkina Faso, Mauritania, Chad, and Niger in an effort to drawdown its troops in Africa in the early 2000s; James Allen, "Soldiers in Africa Get French Commando Training," U.S. Army, press release, February 9, 2007.

[24] "Operation Shader: All You Need to Know About Britain's Fight Against IS," Forces.net, webpage, June 22, 2021.

[25] Interview with Australian defense official, May 7, 2020.

United Kingdom conducted training with Jordanians and other long-time security partners to enhance their contributions to ISAF. In 2007, NATO established a Special Operations Coordination Center in Brussels to help coordinate training for forces from the Czech Republic, Estonia, and Poland to enable them to participate in ISAF. This center, which evolved into a NATO Special Operations Headquarters, continues to train approximately 1,000 students a year for coalition operations in the Middle East, Africa, and Europe.[26] In other cases, U.S. allies work together with each other—but apart from the United States—to support preparation for coalition operations. For example, Australia often works with New Zealand to prepare for multilateral operations. These events are typically not coordinated with U.S. training or equipping efforts.

Engagement Partnering for Future Shaping

Both the United States and its key allies also engage in SC with third countries to pursue strategic interests focused on long-term competition. The objectives for these activities tend to be (1) building partner capacity to shape and maintain regional stability or to prepare for possible operations, (2) increasing access or influence in key geographic areas, and (3) improving U.S. and allied strategic competitiveness vis-à-vis other global actors. Most SC engagements with third parties occur bilaterally, but in recent years initiatives have been undertaken to coordinate allied efforts.

Building Partner Capacity for Future Operations

The United States and its European allies have placed greater emphasis on building partner capacity for engaging in conventional military operations since 2014. U.S. Section 333 SC capacity-building projects in the U.S. European Command have increasingly been targeted at the Eastern European flank. Germany, the United Kingdom, and Canada have also increased their contributions to partnership capacity building through their leadership of Enhanced Forward Presence battlegroups in Lithuania, Estonia, and Latvia,

---

[26] Jim Dorschner and Andrew White, "Quiet Professionals: NATO Special Operations Comes of Age," *Jane's Defence Weekly*, June 25, 2015.

respectively.[27] Other efforts include TACET, which was created by Germany and the United States to synchronize military training and exercises in the Baltic states and Poland, and the Combined Joint Enhanced Training Initiative, which provides coordinated training in Bulgaria and Romania.[28] These initiatives have evolved into other efforts, such as the Capability Enhancement Regional Symposium, a multilateral forum in which NATO allies and key partners share regional situational awareness and visibility on their bilateral activities with the Baltic states and Poland. The Capability Enhancement Regional Symposium has been focused on evolving threats, such as multidomain awareness and cyber security.[29]

U.S. capacity-building efforts in the Pacific region are growing as well, with dedicated funding toward building ally and partner maritime security capabilities. The Philippines, Vietnam, Indonesia, and Malaysia are examples of participants in the South East Asia Maritime Security Initiative. The Army's Pacific Pathways program has included bilateral (and some multinational) exercises with Indonesia, Japan, Korea, Malaysia, Philippines, Singapore, and Thailand to build partner capacity.[30]

These efforts were strengthened by coordinated regional engagements with Australia, Japan, and South Korea to build maritime security and domain awareness in the region. As with the United States, many of the partner capacity-building efforts undertaken by Australia and other highly capable allies are conducted on a bilateral basis. Examples include engagements by the Australian Defence Force to train the Armed Forces of the Philippines on countering complex urban terrorist tactics and maritime

---

[27] The United States also leads an enhanced Forward Presence battlegroup in Poland; Ministry of Foreign Affairs of the Republic of Latvia, "NATO Enhanced Forward Presence," briefing slide, July 25, 2019; and NATO, "NATO Enhanced Forward Presence: 4 Multinational Battle Groups," briefing slide, January 21, 2020a.

[28] We discuss these examples in more detail in Chapter Four.

[29] Email exchange with U.S. defense official, February 28, 2020.

[30] Abby Doll, Angela O'Mahony, Craig A. Bond, Samuel Absher, Jonathan Cham, Jennifer D. P. Moroney, Diana Y. Myers, and Max Steiner, *Assessing the Benefits and Costs of the Pacific Pathways Exercise Series*, RAND Corporation: Santa Monica, Calif., forthcoming. Not available to the general public.

border protection for a recently established Australia-Singapore military training initiative.

Gaining Access and Influence

SC efforts to pursue access and influence with partner nations also are most often conducted bilaterally between the United States (or the U.S. ally) and a third country. The ability to maintain bases, or overflight in the case of a potential contingency, is an underlying objective of many types of U.S. SC engagements, although these objectives and the plans in which they are stated often are not openly shared with even the closest allies because of security classification issues. Australia has made more explicit reference to its objectives in announcing its "Pacific Step Up" program in a 2016 defense white paper.[31] The Step Up program dedicated 2 billion Australian dollars to compete with China for influence, declaring that the Australian Defence Force would "continue to seek to be the principal security partner for Papua New Guinea, Timor-Leste, and Pacific Island countries" by making investments in their militaries and economies.[32] Japan has also initiated a "Free and Open Indo-Pacific" program that invests in 26 SC programs at a cost of over 500 million yen, with a goal, at least in part, to "ensure a rules-based international order including the rule of law, freedom of navigation and overflight."[33]

The objective of improving strategic competitiveness is closely related to that of increasing access and influence, as strategic competitiveness is generally viewed as a contest between great powers. U.S. defense policy has become more focused on the strategic contest with Russia and China since 2018. This is also the case for highly capable allies, although many countries in Europe are obviously more concerned about Russia and countries

---

[31] Australian Government Department of Defence, *2016 Defence White Paper*, Canberra, 2016.

[32] Australia announced that it would invest $144 million to build a Coral Sea Cable System with the Solomon Islands (China is creating a similar system); Grant Wyeth, "Australia's Pacific Step-Up: More Than Just Talk," *The Diplomat*, February 8, 2019.

[33] The Free and Open Indo-Pacific program is a unilateral effort, but Japan reports that it wants to coordinate with regional partners and the United States; Ministry of Foreign Affairs of Japan, "Free and Open Indo-Pacific," briefing, undated.

in the Pacific are more concerned about China. Therefore, NATO countries coordinate most closely on engagements with East European partners and Australia and Japan with neighboring countries.

As a close ally, the United Kingdom coordinates on issues of access and influence more broadly through the U.S.-British Strategic Effects and Alignment Board. The United Kingdom and France also coordinate on African issues with the United States through the Multilateral Planning Group, tri-chaired by the United States, France, and the United Kingdom, which was designed to discuss and synchronize efforts on the continent.[34] France is particularly engaged in West Africa and coordinates with its efforts to maintain influence in the region. U.S. Africa Command also addresses issues of global power competition with 15 international partners that are embedded within its command staff as part of the Multinational Coordination Center.[35]

Conclusions

Focusing on shared SC objectives can set the stage for more productive discussions of how the United States can engage with its allies in preparing for current and future operations and engaging together in third countries of mutual interest. Applying the analytic framework introduced in this chapter can help clarify the issues that the United States and allies should consider as they prioritize their SC activities with each other. Chapter Three provides a more detailed analysis of SC with highly capable allies on current and future operational partnering, and Chapter Four examines SC and coordination with highly capable allies for engagement with third countries.

---

[34] Thomas D. Waldhauser, "Statement of General Thomas D. Waldhauser, United States Marine Corps Commander, United States Africa Command, Before the Senate Committee on Armed Services," Washington, D.C., February 7, 2019.

[35] Thomas D. Waldhauser, "United States Africa Command 2018 Posture Statement," Washington, D.C., March 13, 2018.

Security Cooperation with Highly Capable Allies for Operational Partnering in Iraq, Afghanistan, and Beyond

In this chapter, we provide findings and implications related to the first area of SC with highly capable allies—operational partnering—in the contexts of recent operations in Iraq, Syria, and Afghanistan. We also detail potential opportunities from the perspectives of the United Kingdom and Australia.

We find that explicitly planned SC with highly capable allies for current operations is relatively rare. Formal SC events, such as joint training and planned activities for sharing best practices, are most likely to happen early in an operation. However, mechanisms for sharing lessons can and do emerge organically. In an interview conducted for previous research, one respondent stationed at U.S. Army Europe commented that the allies plan and implement SC only after deployment into theater with other countries.[1] This appears to be particularly true when allied personnel are collocated, when mechanisms such as joint headquarters or liaisons are used, and when unit commands develop strong lines of communication. These mechanisms are generally not considered to be SC but indirectly enable real-time, operationally relevant SC.

In contrast, SC with highly capable allies for future operations is well institutionalized. SC to expand interoperability is a strong focus of U.S. and Army military relationships with these partners and is reinforced through

---

[1] Based on interview conducted for O'Mahony et al., 2017.

development of detailed bilateral plans. These are made possible in part by exchanges of U.S. and allied personnel in each other's service headquarters and major commands, but additional work is required to ensure they are embedded in the right places. However, further opportunities exist for cooperative development of concepts of operations and systems; a lack of systematic U.S. incorporation of allies at the early stages of concept development and onerous restrictions on information sharing currently inhibit cooperation.

Security Cooperation for Operational Partnering with Highly Capable Allies: Recent Operations

As discussed in Chapter One, this report grew out of a request for the RAND Arroyo Center to identify lessons learned for prioritizing SC with highly capable allies based on SC that was undertaken in preparation for and during operations in Iraq, Syria, and Afghanistan. In keeping with this scoping, in this section we focus on recent operations. Although future conflicts might differ significantly from the conflicts in Iraq, Syria, and Afghanistan, we expect these findings will provide valuable insights for the Army as it prepares for potential competition and conflict with near-peer adversaries as well as lesser contingencies.

The findings in this section reflect SC for operational partnering in current operations. These tend to include SC to

1.   improve capabilities for current operations
2.   share information for current operations
3.   develop workarounds.

Our main findings regarding how well the United States and its highly capable allies use SC to operate together more effectively fall into two categories. The first captures the quality and quantity of SC that occurs during operations. In recent operations in Iraq and Afghanistan, there appeared to be consistently low use of SC to prepare individual countries' forces for operations or to promote information sharing within operations. When it came to working together, U.S., British, and Australian forces either relied on procedures and understandings that had been developed through earlier interactions or they developed workarounds.

Second, problems that U.S., British, and Australian forces encountered when working together often stemmed from inadequate operational planning, differing strategic priorities, and political disagreements on how to approach operations—sources of disagreement that might be less amenable to mitigation through SC than simple gaps at the operational or tactical levels. Overall, coalition difficulties, disagreements and failures in Iraq during OIF and Afghanistan during OEF have been well-documented.[2] These differences limit what can be achieved through SC for operational partnering; SC can provide mechanisms to smooth operational partnering, but it is insufficient to overcome the problems engendered by political disagreements and poor planning.

Most Predeployment Training to Improve Capabilities Has Been Conducted Unilaterally

U.S., British, and Australian units' predeployment training tended to be unilateral in preparing for coalition operations in Iraq and Afghanistan during the past two decades. Predeployment training at Hohenfels in Germany was mostly geared toward less capable allies, especially those in Eastern Europe and the Caucasus. We found very little evidence in the historical accounts of OIF, OEF, and more-recent operations or in G-TSCMIS entries that the United States and its highly capable allies trained together before deployment to the field. A campaign study of Operation HERRICK in Afghanistan conducted by the British Army's Directorate of Land Warfare touts "the inclusion of both joint and multinational partners throughout the training

---

[2] See John Chilcot, *The Report of the Iraq Inquiry*, London: National Archives, July 6, 2016; Joel D. Rayburn and Frank K. Sobchak, eds., *The U.S. Army in the Iraq War, Volume 1: Invasion, Insurgency, Civil War, 2003–2006*, Carlisle, Pa.: Strategic Studies Institute and U.S. Army War College Press, January 2019a; Joel D. Rayburn and Frank K. Sobchak, eds., *The U.S. Army in the Iraq War, Volume 2: Surge and Withdrawal, 2007–2011*, Carlisle, Pa.: Strategic Studies Institute and U.S. Army War College Press, January 2019b; Theo Farrell, *Unwinnable: Britain's War in Afghanistan, 2001–2014*, London: Bodley Head, 2017; and Alexander Powell, Larry Lewis, Catherine Norman, and Jerry Meyerle, *Summary Report: U.S.-UK Integration in Helmand*, Arlington, Va.: Center for Naval Analysis, February 2016.

progression" for increased operational capability, but it does not reference any specific event. The same study also states that "during much of Operation HERRICK, formations, units and individuals often found themselves deploying without having trained with . . .organisations [sic]) such as allies," and as a result, "did not fully understand how to operate with or alongside other organisations [sic] or capabilities—all of which carried potential risks."[3]

Conversely, British and Australian personnel involved in operations in Iraq and Afghanistan suggested that, although some joint predeployment training would have been helpful, they did not perceive the absence of such training to be particularly damaging to their units' abilities to work together with allies.[4] There was broad agreement among interviewees that robust predeployment SC—strategic and operational planning, training, and exercises—would not be necessary given previous decades of operational experience and SC. As one British interviewee stated, British forces "expected simply to roll under the U.S. plan" in Afghanistan.[5]

Interviewees' belief that U.S., British, and Australian forces were able to work well together on the ground, despite lack of predeployment training, appears to be well-founded based on documented experiences in Iraq and Afghanistan. In Iraq, late 2003 coalition cooperation to address the IED problem was a particularly successful example of cooperation in the field between the United States, the United Kingdom, and the Australians. IEDs quickly emerged as the primary killer of coalition forces in postinvasion Iraq. Disparate coalition units had been working on their own counter-IED measures until special operators merged British, U.S., and Australian ordnance specialists and technicians into a Combined Explosives Exploitation

---

[3]   British Army, *Operation HERRICK Campaign Study*, Warminster, March 2015, pp. 5.1_3 and 5.1_4. The chapter devoted to training in this study includes a table of eight major predeployment training exercises that supported Operation HERRICK. Each of these exercises took place in the United Kingdom and there is no reference to U.S. or other coalition participation.

[4]   The CNA report was somewhat less sanguine, stating that delays in British force development limited the amount of predeployment training that took place with U.S. forces and degraded the ability to work together effectively. See Powell et al., 2016.

[5]   Author interview with senior British defense officials, December 2019.

Cell (later incorporated into Combined Joint Task Force TROY). In Afghanistan, after years of adopting a "defensive mindset" in avoiding IEDs, the 2008 Burley Review determined that the United Kingdom should adopt a more assertive approach similar to the United States, which used intelligence resources to target the networks planting IEDs. This resulted in the establishment of Task Force Torchlight at Camp Bastion and Task Force Varsity in Kandahar.[6]

Similarly, U.S. and British forces shared a defined battlespace in Helmand Province between 2009 and 2014, with contiguous areas of responsibility that required coordinating targeting and operational missions. Despite the absence of any predeployment training, and in the face of a high level of ongoing personnel turnover,[7] British and American personnel developed a robust level of operational coordination. In 2010, the United States and United Kingdom integrated their national aviation efforts in Regional Command Southwest to form an integrated staff.[8] In 2013, they did the same for targeting efforts, forming the Coalition Targeting Cell. A British Army study on Operation HERRICK credits the former as "perhaps the best model for coalition integration."[9] By 2012, U.S. and British forces had even combined their targeting efforts into a joint operations center.

In all these examples, it took time for the partners to develop effective mechanisms for working together. Forces face a tradeoff between planning and training together before an operation and developing workarounds on the ground. Reducing the severity of this tradeoff ought to be a fundamental goal of steady state SC (i.e., SC conducted for future shaping). Moreover, in a high-intensity conflict against a regional power or near-peer actor, there might be no time to develop workarounds, given the importance of first battles and potential for rapid escalation.

---

[6] Farrell, 2017, p. 344.

[7] British and U.S. units' arrival and departure from theater did not align. Moreover, at the time, the United Kingdom relied on individual augmentees for command staff billets, which limited opportunities to participate in predeployment efforts; Powell, 2016, p. 14.

[8] Powell, 2016, p. 9.

[9] British Army, 2015, pp. 1-2_5.

As the Army prepares for the possibility of near-peer conflict and focuses on increasing its expeditionary agility, developing and maintaining the ability to interoperate quickly and effectively with highly capable allies will become increasingly important. A key reason that U.S., British, and Australian personnel have been able to work together so well in recent operations is the steady state interactions between these allies, ranging from high-level embeds, multinational exercises (e.g., joint warfighter exercises), education and training programs,[10] and officer and unit exchange programs (e.g., the Military Personnel Exchange Program). However, the British Army explicitly states that the integration skills jointly developed during nearly five years in Afghanistan are perishable and that a comprehensive defense engagement program to preserve these lessons should be developed: "The challenge during this fallow period before the next coalition operation is how to start the next operation as an integrated coalition, capitalising [sic] on those coalition synergies from the start."[11]

Implications

Given the relative dearth of SC activities during ongoing operations, the low likelihood that these will become more common in future operations, and the importance of steady-state SC activities for preparing units and personnel to work together rapidly and effectively in the absence of predeployment training, we identified the following implications:

- **Steady state SC activities between the United States and highly capable allies should continue to focus on providing opportunities for developing and exercising operational partnering.** As discussed, such efforts are a central aspect of security relationships between the United States and its closest partners. These activities should emphasize not only developing soldiers' skills and familiarity but also developing procedures for shared communications, processes, and logistics. Waiting until an operation occurs is too late to develop operational partnerships.

---

[10] For example, every British Army major spends two weeks training at Fort Leavenworth.

[11] British Army, 2015, pp. 1-2_6.

- **Mission-essential tasks related to multinational interoperability should be considered for steady-state U.S. unit training to enable swift, effective operational partnering.** For units that engage in multinational training, incorporating interoperability and operational partnering into unit mission-essential task lists could help ensure that the appropriate activities are highlighted in exercises with highly capable allies that prepare them to work together not only in near-peer conflicts, but also contingency operations in other contexts.[12]

United States and Allies Share Information, But Only Opportunistically

At a basic level, most SC is about sharing information. Although most information sharing through SC occurs outside ongoing operations, we analyzed activities that were designed to share lessons with highly capable partners during operations in Iraq and Afghanistan. As with predeployment training, formally organized cooperative activities to share operationally relevant lessons were rare. That said, throughout our research, we sought examples that demonstrated how valuable it was for U.S., British, and Australian forces to share operational lessons with each other. A few representative examples stand out.

As previously mentioned, the United States and United Kingdom occupied a shared battlespace in Afghanistan's Regional Command Southwest and integrated their air and targeting efforts to prevent seams and help optimize support for ground forces. At a more micro level, U.S. and British personnel consistently shared lessons learned and incorporated them into their evolving TTPs. For instance, a procedure routinely used by Royal Navy pilots that was seen as good operational practice was adopted by the rest of the United Kingdom's Joint Aviation Group as well as the U.S. Marine Corps' Air Combat Element, which extended to briefing formats and general

---

[12] For concepts on how such mission-essential tasks might be incorporated and measured in U.S. Army units, see Bryan W. Hallmark, Christopher G. Pernin, Andrea M. Abler, Ryan Haberman, Sale Lilly, Samantha McBirney, Angela O'Mahony, and Erik E. Mueller, *An Analysis of Alternative Approaches to Measuring Mutltinational Interoperability: Early Development of the Army Interoperability Measurement System (AIMS)*, Santa Monica, Calif.: RAND Corporation, RR-A617-1, 2021.

mission business.[13] U.S. Marines deployed to Regional Command Southwest credited the United Kingdom with helping them refine their targeting practices, particularly how best to use the varying capabilities of multiple intelligence, surveillance, and reconnaissance platforms tasked with tracking one or a group of potential targets.[14]

Given that distribution of lessons learned within the Army—much less at the joint and combined force levels—is highly problematic,[15] these types of information-sharing activities tended to emerge organically rather than as part of an institutionalized sharing process. When we followed up with operators on how lessons tended to be shared, we were told that information sharing generally occurred through three pathways. First, personnel found themselves in the same place at the same time and informally discussed their operational experiences with each other—that is, they "talked shop." Second, if personnel were aware of each other's operations, they might reach out for insights in the face of current challenges. Third, embedded partner personnel would act as formal or informal liaisons to share lessons with personnel from both countries. Operators noted that sharing lessons was helpful, but it generally only occurred opportunistically. This raises the concern that fewer lessons are shared with allies than is optimal during operations.

On the other hand, the Combined Joint Task Force in OIR experienced severe difficulty formally sharing information among coalition partners, largely because of differing communication systems and problems with classification. It was not until the joint operations center began to use Global Command and Control System–Joint that coalition personnel could fully see the required common operational picture needed for the operation. An insight reported by the Center for Army Lessons Learned suggested that

---

[13] British Army, 2015, pp. 1-2_5.

[14] U.S. Marines, interview with the author, Camp Leatherneck, Helmand, Afghanistan, April–May 2013.

[15] Stephen Watts, Christopher M. Schnaubelt, Sean Mann, Angela O'Mahony, and Michael Schwille, *Pacific Engagement: Forging Tighter Connections Between Tactical Security Cooperation Activities and U.S. Strategic Goals in the Asia-Pacific Region*, Santa Monica, Calif.: RAND Corporation, RR-1920-A, 2018.

plans for information sharing across the coalition should be in place before an operation starts.[16]

When we asked interview respondents about potential shortcomings in operationally relevant information sharing, many thought that developing a mechanism for sharing operationally relevant observations across coalition partners would be useful—particularly if these mechanisms were made available to units prior to deployment.

Implications

Documenting lessons learned and sharing information between different offices and across time is a perennial challenge for the Army. Our first two implications focus on enabling bottom-up communications between units undertaking similar missions of operating in similar environments. The third and fourth focus on shared communications infrastructure:

- **Develop updated guidance for deployed U.S. units on lessons learned for communications with allied units.** Communications sometimes happen naturally in an operational setting. However, the Army could formalize guidance to deployed units on identifying allied counterpart units that have conducted or are conducting similar operations in the combined battlespace and initiating interactions designed to share experiences. Such exchanges could help each unit address challenges that have arisen during operations.
- **In instances in which the United States and an ally have developed clear interoperability workarounds in the field, ensure that they are incorporated into interoperability plans and roadmaps.** Successful workarounds are important to capture and archive for use in future operations and exercises with the ally; they could also be improved and expanded to include other allies.
- **Formal, preestablished information-sharing mechanisms should be in place to increase lines of communication on combined lessons learned during operations.** DoD efforts toward establishing and exer-

---

[16] Center for Army Lessons Learned, *Initial Impressions Report—ARCENT Transition to Combined Joint Task Force-Operation Inherent Resolve*, Fort Leavenworth, Kan., March 2016.

cising mission partner environments can serve as the foundation for a shared communications network.[17]

- **Capturing allied lessons learned would be useful as part of the Joint Lessons Learned Information System.** Building a separate allies and partners lessons learned information system might be unnecessary; including such a lessons learned portal as part of an operational communications infrastructure might be useful. Within this portal, providing a template for contributing observations and a list of common topics for tagging observations would increase the value of captured data.

Sharing Personnel Is a Valuable Means of Operational Coordination and Workarounds but Is Not a Substitute for Combined Operational Planning

There are three different concepts for sharing personnel between allies: *liaisons* (who work for their home country but are positioned in a foreign country's structure to help with information flow), *personnel exchanges* (one-for-one exchanges of personnel between two countries), and *embeds* (who serve in a foreign country in a foreign billet, usually in a position of prominence). It is worth noting that liaisons are often excluded from sensitive conversations because they are seen as representing their home countries. Exchanges and embeds might experience some of this, but because they are essentially serving in U.S. billets, they are more likely to be accepted and included in these conversations. Liaisons and personnel exchanges are an important part of U.S. SC in steady state. These exchanges are designed to encourage collaboration, create personal relationships between allied personnel, impart knowledge, and enhance strategic partnerships. Continuing with the theme of operationalizing SC, during operations, allies provide personnel to joint headquarters and liaison officers to individual units and headquarters. These personnel provide valuable channels for communica-

---

[17] As noted in Pernin, 2020, "the military's push to a common 'mission partner environment' aims to have wide partner inclusion and offer key services necessary to execute mission command functions in a multinational environment. The extent to which this is tested against actual partner capabilities or in specific contexts and scenarios will of course be a critical signpost of its eventual utility."

tion, coordination, and cooperation.[18] Interviewees highlighted liaisons' problem-solving capabilities during operations—in particular, their abilities to develop workarounds.

However, during operations in Iraq and Afghanistan, historical accounts and interviewee comments identified the following shortcomings to relying on liaisons:

- Liaisons were not always available. Staffing liaison positions was often not a priority for units.
- Liaisons were valuable, but they were not a replacement for a robust communications network, a common operating picture, or joint planning.
- Not all embedded partner personnel are tasked or trained as liaisons, even if they liaise informally. Relying on nonliaison embedded personnel meant relying on informal points of contact and took time away from completing assigned tasks. This was less of a problem when working with Five Eye partners, but liaisons' effectiveness still was limited by their inability to access classified information.

Operations in Iraq and Afghanistan demonstrated that formal coordination cells and headquarters were more effective, if more resource-intensive, than using liaisons. Formal coordination cells were established at the onset of OIR. Beginning in May 2014, U.S. Special Forces Command created an International Directorate to integrate partner nations into special operations forces planning for multilateral courses of action. U.S. Central Command then established a Combined Joint Forces Land Component Command–Iraq in 2015, which enabled command and control of coalition forces supporting OIR.[19] Building upon lessons learned from past operations, the Combined Joint Forces Land Component Command–Iraq (later renamed

---

[18] In operations in Iraq in 2007, liaison officers were relied upon heavily for coordination; however, this information-sharing process was slow and did not achieve the intended unity of effort or speed of command to deliver the required operational effects; Martin M. Westphal and Thomas C. Lang, "Conducting Operations in a Mission Partner Environment," *Joint Force Quarterly*, July 2014.

[19] Lessons Learned Operations and Strategic Studies Branch, 2015.

Combined Joint Task Force–OIR) was able to share information with a combined enterprise regional information exchange. According to a 2015 Joint Staff report, U.S. Central Command's integration of military members from the allied countries early in their planning for the situation in Syria and Iraq played an important role in the coordination of operations.[20]

Implications

We identified three implications for improving effective operational partnering through the use of liaisons and synchronized coalition operations:

- **Liaison capabilities should be planned for at the outset of coalition operations—not as an afterthought.** Operational plans should include manning requirements that ensure appropriate liaison staffing as part of coalition command and operations structures. Notably, working with liaisons is a skill. Units that are expected to operate with coalition partners should consider how to work effectively with liaisons in those units' mission essential tasks. Establishing coordination cells with liaisons can be effective in improving planning and communication for such quickly evolving operations as OIR.
- **Include tasks into multinational exercises that require working with liaisons.** In further efforts to "train as you fight," recent exercises have prioritized developing skills with technical modes for coalition communications (i.e., mission partner environment). Multinational exercises should also continue to develop human modes (i.e., liaisons) for coalition communications.
- **Stand up joint multinational planning structures early in a coalition operation.** Liaisons are valuable but are not a replacement for joint multinational planning structures. Joint headquarters, coordination cells, and joint communications networks are more robust than relying on liaisons for planning, communicating about, and coordinating coalition operations.

---

[20] Deployable Training Division, Joint Staff J7, *Insights and Best Practices Focus Paper: Forming a JTF HQ*, Suffolk, Va., September 2015.

Coordination Among Allies Affected Less by Geography Than by the "Thickness" of Battlespace Lines

The previous three findings dealt directly with SC for operational partnering during ongoing operations; the remaining two address structural conditions that limit the amount of SC that will occur.

SC activities, such as sharing lessons learned, are less likely to occur when coalition partner missions are organized geographically, not functionally, and if partners are assigned sequestered battlespaces with minimal, if any, routinized coordination. This might represent the greatest gap in cooperation during operations, as partners are often trying to accomplish the same missions and facing the same challenges but have fewer opportunities to share information than if they were operating in the same battlespace. Once a theater of operations is divided along firm geographic lines, there are fewer organic opportunities for engagement. If such divisions must be drawn, engagement in SC with allies to ensure proper communication and coordination is necessary.

Geographical division of the theater is a common organizational structure for coalition operations and might be more likely in the presence of political differences. This was the case in Iraq, where British forces were in command of and largely concentrated in Basra Province in the far south of the country and adopted concepts of operations and a set of TTPs different from those of their U.S. counterparts elsewhere in the country. This was a source of frustration on both sides, as coalition partners carried out separate, and sometimes contradictory, approaches in their respective areas of operation. The Chilcot Report and the U.S. Army History of the Iraq War both describe the disjointedness of the geographically divided coalition approaches in Iraq. "In the absence of a coherent strategy," the Chilcot Report explains, "coalition partners continued to work independently of one another." It continues:

> U.S. and [British] strategies for Iraq began to diverge almost immediately after the conflict. Although the differences were managed, by early 2007 the United Kingdom was finding it difficult to play down the divergence, which was, by that point, striking.[21]

---

[21] Chilcot, 2016, Executive Summary, p. 124.

The geographic division of labor "uncoupled most of southern Iraq from the broader U.S. military campaign." As time went by,

> [Multinational Division Southeast] MND-SE became increasingly disconnected from Multi-National Corps-Iraq's planning and operations, with both the U.S. command in Baghdad and the British command in Basra operating as though events in central Iraq and far southern Iraq were unrelated.[22]

In Afghanistan, the delineation between assigned U.S. and British geographic battlespaces occurred at the district level and was demarcated by more of a dotted line in that operations were coordinated, and command staffs were mixed. U.S. and British forces combined air assets, eventually merged targeting cells, and even adjusted shared TTPs based on lessons learned. These moves both helped close seams between assigned districts and made for a smoother transition when U.S. Marines eventually took over responsibility of northern and southern districts from British forces.

Implication

As demonstrated by U.S., British, and Australian experiences in Iraq and Afghanistan, both operationally and politically, geographic separation of areas of responsibility will remain a common strategy, even as advances in interoperability make it easier to envision operational planning that divides forces by functional area within shared areas of control. This need not, however, prevent close coordination and cooperation at the operational level. The findings discussed in this section suggest the following implication:

- **When coalition forces are geographically separated, information sharing will need to be actively pursued to identify lessons to be learned from coalition partners' operations.** SC is much less likely to emerge organically when coalition forces are geographically separated in designated areas separated by a "thick" line of demarcation and operating under distinct authorities and TTPs. In contrast, SC is more likely to emerge organically when coalition forces are operating in con-

---

[22] Rayburn and Sobchak, 2019b.

tiguous battlespaces separated by a "dotted" line and operating under similar or identical authorities and TTPs. Such conditions encourage increased coordination and the pursuit of mutually beneficial cooperation. Senior leader engagements might help catalyze this.

Differing Political Priorities Are a Major Constraint on Effective Partnering

Our final finding regarding operational partnering in recent operations is that political disagreements can have deleterious effects on operational partnering. This clearly occurred during OIF. The United States wanted to pursue expansive goals throughout the operation, but the United Kingdom's appetite for continuing its intervention in Iraq waned as domestic opposition to British participation waxed:

> [T]he British public and even some within the British Government questioned the legality of continuing the conflict beyond the invasion and expressed a great aversion to British casualties. Increasingly, British officials began to view the war as a political risk that needed to be minimized by limiting the British military's exposure.[23]

British and U.S. operations became increasingly disconnected.

Political differences between the United States and Australia were less acute, but also limited the range of operations Australia was willing to undertake. Australian Train Advise Assist Command–Air officials and Australian military historians consistently stated that Australia was in Afghanistan for the purpose of supporting the United States (while minimizing costs to Australian forces). As one respondent noted,

> Australia is the only winner of the Iraq War. Australia had two goals in Iraq. The first goal was to cozy up to the [United States]. The second

---

[23] Justin Maciejewski, "'Best Effort': Operation Sinbad and the Iraq Campaign," in Jonathan Bailey, Richard Iron, and Hew Strachan, eds., *British Generals in Blair's Wars*, Surrey, United Kingdom: Ashgate Publishing, 2013.

goal was to do as little as possible. We accomplished both with flying colors.[24]

Another respondent noted that

[w]e didn't do a lot in Iraq and then tried to leave before the embarrassment of Phase IV took over. We were shamed into coming back but then tried to do even less during the war. Australia really was the ant dodging the two elephants of the [United States] and the [United Kingdom] in this conflict.[25]

Overall, political differences and national caveats can be critical barriers to operational integration and synchronization. For example, the Germans were quite restricted during OEF in terms of the conditions under which they could operate in a combat environment. German forces were reportedly not permitted to leave their operating bases after dark and, when they could, they were prohibited from leaving the base without an ambulance in the convoy.[26] In one of the more extreme cases in 2009, the German military called in an air strike in Kunduz Province on a group of tanker trucks that had been hijacked and abandoned by insurgents. However, the Germans' restrictive caveats prevented them from approaching the area where the trucks had been abandoned to investigate more closely before calling in the strike. Because of this, they were unaware that the trucks were surrounded not by militants but by civilians collecting the fuel spilling out of the fuel tanks. The strike led to the deaths of 90 to 150 Afghan civilians.[27]

---

[24] Author interview with senior Australian and British defense officials, Russell Headquarters, Canberra, Australia, May and November 2019. See also Albert Palazzo, *The Australian Army and the War in Iraq: 2002–2010*, Canberra: Australian Army, March 2011.

[25] Author interview with senior Australian and British defense officials, 2019.

[26] Ahmed Rashid, *Descent Into Chaos: The United States and the Failure of Nation Building in Pakistan, Afghanistan, and Central Asia*, New York: Viking Press, 2008, p. 354.

[27] Constantin Schüßler and Yee-Kuang Heng, "The Bundeswehr and the Kunduz Airstrike 4 September 2009: Germany's Post-Heroic Moment?" *European Security*, Vol. 22, No. 3, August 2013, pp. 355–375.

Differing national caveats are less structurally constricting but also limit effective operational partnering. This frustration was particularly acute in Afghanistan, especially after the ISAF mission was elevated to a four-star U.S.-led command; at times, more than 40 NATO allies and partners participated there under varying national caveats. General Dan McNeill, ISAF's first four-star commander, reportedly kept a list of each nation's caveats above his desk and once complained, "Caveats preclude you from planning a military operation to its most effective and efficient state."[28] For the United Kingdom and Australia, however, formal caveats rarely (if ever) came into play; each country committed its forces to full-spectrum operations. There were, however, instances of national-focused criticism at the operational level.

There was some political controversy over where the bulk of British forces would be deployed as the NATO mission spread to the more volatile southern part of the country in 2006. Kandahar, as the most populous and strategically important province in that region, appeared to be an ideal fit for the British. However, Canada, eager to shed a reputation of being proficient only for peacekeeping, insisted on taking the lead as a condition of agreeing to deploy to the south. This left the United Kingdom to accept the assignment in neighboring Helmand and perhaps created some hard feelings that U.S. leadership was not more supportive. As Nick Beadle, the private secretary to the British Defence Secretary at the time, stated,

> How did we end up going to Helmand rather than Kandahar? I can offer nothing more as a reason than a failure to persuade the [United States] to support us . . . the [United States] rightly guessed that we would go into southern Afghanistan anyway.[29]

Fair or not, there were a handful of cases in Helmand in which U.S. military personnel were critical of what they viewed as a lack of British assertiveness and a reluctance to support U.S. objectives. Major General Ben Freakley, commander of U.S. Joint Task Force 76 in 2006 through 2007, expressed

---

[28] Dan K. McNeill, videoconference of interview with Bryan Whitman, U.S. Department of Defense, June 5, 2007.

[29] Farrell, 2017, p. 142.

frustration over what he viewed a "lackluster performance" on the part of the British in the south; when stretched British forces in Helmand refused to devote resources to U.S.-led counterterrorism operations, he implored British leadership to "Get off your asses!"[30] Later, when the U.S. Marines were taking over responsibility of some of Helmand's northern districts from British forces, one U.S. officer asked, "They were here for four years. What did they do?"[31]

To some extent, this operational discord was an extension of a command structure that political authorities prevented from operating in a traditional manner. With multinational commanding officers at various echelons beholden both to their superior officers and national capitals, friction was inevitable. As Farrell argues, "It would have been hard to design a more convoluted and dysfunctional command structure for British forces."[32]

Implication

We derived the following implication of the complicating presence of national caveats in coalition operations:

- **Planning processes need to identify areas of disagreement and constraints caused by national caveats and subsequent differences in operational priorities.** Political differences will often introduce severe complexities into coalition operations. SC among participating allies outside the theater of operations should focus on how these caveats might impact operations, and how the coalition should address the resulting challenges—before these complications are experienced in the field.

---

[30] Farrell, 2017, p. 179.

[31] Farrell, 2017, p. 356.

[32] Farrell, 2017, p. 170.

Security Cooperation for Operational Partnering with Highly Capable Allies: Future Shaping

Operational partnering for future shaping is about conducting SC with highly capable allies focused on capability-development and interoperability to enhance the effectiveness of future coalition operations. Therefore, our findings draw more heavily on our interviews with U.S., British, and Australian stakeholders than on lessons from Iraq, Syria and Afghanistan.

The findings in this section reflect the upper right cell in the framework discussed in Chapter Two—SC for operational partnering for future shaping. This tends to

1. improve interoperability for future operations
2. establish shared standards and procedures
3. aid codevelopment of capabilities.

Currently, for the United States, United Kingdom, and Australia— and other U.S. highly capable allies—all three of these SC objectives are focused, directly or indirectly, on interoperability. As a result, our main findings revolve around prioritizing, developing, and sustaining multinational interoperability. The United States, United Kingdom, and Australia are investing heavily in interoperability—as evidenced through new strategy and planning documents and through key bilateral and multilateral exercises.[33] It is also the case that key barriers remain, some of which the Army cannot resolve because they reside at higher policy levels. However, the Army can highlight their importance and help address them.

Security Cooperation to Expand Interoperability Is a Strong Focus of U.S.-Allied Military Relationships

Allies such as the United Kingdom and Australia support and encourage interoperability discussions and new investments during senior-level interactions with the Army. For example, interoperability discussions have historically dominated the agenda for the U.S.-British army-to-army staff

---

[33] This is discussed in detail in Chapter Five.

talks. The Multinational Fusion Cell in the HQDA brings together assigned personnel from multiple allied countries (the United Kingdom, Australia, Japan, Germany, France, and others) to focus on interoperability and to develop U.S.-allied bilateral interoperability roadmaps. Standing organizations, such as ABCANZ, also exist to work through interoperability issues at the operational level. Large-scale exercises, such as the aforementioned biannual Talisman Sabre series between the United States and Australia, are very much focused on addressing interoperability challenges identified from recent operations and planning for future operations. NATO defines interoperability along three dimensions—human, procedural, and technical—which is a helpful way to categorize interoperability challenges.[34] We find general agreement among our interlocutors that SC with highly capable allies to support human, procedural, and technical interoperability is advancing at the operational and tactical levels, but there is concern about a lack of multiyear funding and programming to guide longer-term planning for multinational interoperability exercises.[35]

Despite this focus, interoperability initiatives at the strategic level have been relatively *ad hoc* from allies' perspectives. The Army's Interoperability Campaign Plan frames and institutionalizes interoperability efforts internally and operationalizes it with designated partners. Allies support the Army's focus on interoperability writ large, but the links between interoperability planning and ongoing SC activities needs to be stronger. As an example, the GORT, a bilateral event between the United States and the United Kingdom at the three- and four-star level, is not explicitly linked to the discussions that occur at the one- and two-star levels. According to key allied officials, issues raised at the GORT level should be automatically addressed at the subsequent Army staff talks (ASTs) and drive the discussions at the lower level working groups. Interoperability issues and priorities raised at the GORTs/staff talks should also be linked to other key bilateral SC activities, creating a real battle rhythm for interoperability.

Moreover, allies have suggested that although bilateral vision statements for interoperability—such as the emerging one with the United Kingdom—

---

[34] NATO, "Interoperability: Connecting NATO Forces," webpage, last updated March 24, 2020b.

[35] Written comment of senior Army official, received October 1, 2020.

are positive steps, their language could be made stronger and clearer. They suggest dropping the term *vision* and making bilateral *campaign* plans. In addition, aspirational verbs in Army plans, such as *institutionalize*, should be replaced by stronger verbs, such as *guarantee*.[36]

Both British and Australian officials talk about wanting to be the United States' partner of choice; the United Kingdom has in place an explicit strategic communications campaign plan that focuses on improved access and science and technology collaboration. For the United Kingdom, this partnering includes such areas as energy; antisubmarine warfare; hypersonics; network command, control, and communications; and nuclear collaboration. For Australia, areas include intelligence, surveillance, and reconnaissance; radars; and other high-technology systems. The emphasis on being a *partner of choice* refers to being capable, likeminded, and *committed*. It is understandable why key allies desire to have the strongest language possible in interoperability planning documents.

Implications

We derived the following implications from our findings on expanding interoperability with the United Kingdom, Australia, and other highly capable allies:

- **Strengthening the links between key SC activities focused on interoperability at the top level to lower echelons will help to ensure that the messages are clear and that appropriate actions are taken at the working group levels.** In this area formal mechanisms for linking the deliberations and decisions made at GORT meetings with activities at the army-to-army staff talks would be helpful.
- **Language in interoperability planning documents could be less aspirational and more definitive.** Not only would this make SC plans for interoperability more concrete for both the United States and its allies, but it would also encourage formulation of measurable goals and metrics for the SC community to enable assessment, monitoring, and evaluation of progress in enhancing that interoperability.

---

[36] Author interviews with senior British defense officials, 2019.

- **Multiyear planning and resourcing for interoperability would help provide predictability to U.S.-allied SC efforts in this area.** The development of bilateral interoperability roadmaps goes a long way to facilitating such multiyear planning and making SC for operational partnering more systematic.

Lessons from Operations Have Driven Interoperability Priorities

The challenges in Iraq and Afghanistan that U.S. and allied forces faced in communicating effectively and sharing intelligence have shaped SC for future operations. The development of the Mission Partner Environment and its incorporation into joint force exercises is a primary example of how lessons from past operations are being incorporated to ensure greater interoperability.[37] The Mission Partner Environment concept stemmed from the desire to create a network infrastructure that employed a single security level network on which the U.S. and partner mission command systems spoke a common language. In multinational exercises, the Army has increasingly focused on allies to streamline coalition data sharing on logistics, terrain, fires, and friendly and enemy position data; to enable U.S. and coalition partners to access the shared Mission Partner Environment network; and to enable more integrated information sharing and a real-time coalition common operating picture.[38]

From the British Army's perspective, a major activity underway is the integration of the 3rd Division and its seven brigades into U.S. Army Third Corps under the Warfighter Exercise series. This will be a full-spectrum integration that includes command and control, planning, current operations, and future operations functions. Both countries are drawing directly upon very specific, tactical-level interoperability lessons from Iraq and Afghanistan to make this happen. For example, one major lesson from recent operations is that logistics systems do not integrate well, which War-

---

[37] Amy Walker, "Army Leverages Joint Multinational Exercises to Speed Network Modernization," U.S. Army, press release, May 1, 2018.

[38] Amy Walker and Justin Eimers, "Multinational Exercises Aim to Improve Coalition Data Sharing," U.S. Army, press release, April 8, 2019.

fighter Exercise scenarios will address. British officials remarked that, as far as predeployment training is concerned, the Warfighter Exercise is the only activity that is required to ensure that the two countries are interoperable from a land forces perspective.[39]

Interoperability priorities have been applied within the rubric of such contingency operations as OIF and OEF, but there has been concern about relying too heavily on the lessons of past operations and "fighting the last war." More-effective communications systems will be critical in preparing for contingencies that might evolve quickly, but the types of communications and intelligence networks needed and used might differ in future conflict scenarios. Allies are concerned that developing networks based only on lessons from previous conflicts could leave the United States and its coalition partners with inadequate means of communicating and sharing intelligence.[40]

Implications

We derived the following implications from our findings that highly capable allies such as Australia and the United Kingdom prioritize improving interoperability with the United States:

- **Future interoperability efforts should be prioritized based on their relevance to expected future operations.** Interoperability is a means to an end, not an end in and of itself.
- **Steady-state SC should build the foundation for agile interoperability.** As previous operations have demonstrated, there is often little time available to build interoperability during a current operation. SC activities, such as warfighter exercises, can develop interoperability processes that set the preconditions for quickly spinning up interoperable operations. Such exercises should seek not only to advance interoperability among combat forces but also among logistics and other support elements. Joint headquarters can also facilitate the development of strong communications and understanding of each ally's TTPs.

---

[39] Author interview with senior British defense officials, 2019.

[40] Author interview with senior British defense officials, 2019.

Embeds, Personnel Exchanges and Liaisons Are Useful—If They Are in the Right Positions

There is a long history of sharing talent between key allies to strengthen relationships and increase understanding of each other's strategies, policies, and processes. Deep relationships built through working "in the trenches" for prolonged periods of time are the main conduits for rapid and accurate information sharing in times of crisis. One strong theme from both the British and Australian case studies was the need to ensure that these embeds, one-for-one personnel changes, and liaisons occupy key positions to enable the very best connectivity possible. British and Australian officials suggested that Army embeds, exchanges, and liaisons (emphasis on the first two) should be placed in such new Army organizations as Army Futures Command and the Security Force Assistance Command. Both noted the importance of sending individuals with a strategy and planning background to these newer posts.[41]

It is equally as important for the Army to work with capable allies to determine which positions in allied countries are absolutely key for Army officials to occupy. For example, Australian officials have remarked that they would like to have more U.S. instructors at the Australian Army command and staff colleges. One senior defense official remarked that the United States needs to learn that although the Australian counterparts very much appreciate and respect their U.S. colleagues, cultural differences exist are sometimes not picked up by the U.S. officials. These nuances include engaging in small talk, avoiding bragging about oneself, and emphasizing informalities in meetings; understanding these nuances is important to promoting interoperability at a human level. Having more U.S. instructors in the key defense colleges would help bridge these cultural gaps. "They [the U.S. military] like us, they aren't like us" was his interesting quote.[42]

HQDA houses a Multinational Fusion Cell in Plans and G2 Intel (G35) that consists of liaisons and exchange officers from the United Kingdom, Australia, France, Canada, Japan, Germany, and a few other countries. Cell

---

[41] Author interview with senior Australian and British defense officials, 2019; author interview with senior British defense officials, 2019.

[42] Author interview with senior Australian and British defense officials, 2019.

staff have been working on a variety of projects aimed at improving coalition interoperability, including bilateral interoperability roadmaps. It is not clear that groups (foreigners housed separately together) such as these are more useful than individuals in key positions, but it will be worth following the accomplishments of the Multinational Fusion Cell.

The British Army has an interesting and unique relationship with Army Command and General Staff College at Ft. Leavenworth. Every British Army major attends a two-week training course in the United States. The idea is to instill in young majors relatively early in their career the importance of working alongside the Army as part of a coalition. The Army only provides this opportunity to the British Army, although theoretically, this invitation could be expanded to other countries as resources allow.

Implications

We identified the following two implications from our exploration of U.S.-allied embeds, personnel exchanges, and liaisons:

- **The United States should work closely with highly capable allies to identify and prioritize the most-appropriate billets for exchanges and high level embeds.** Opportunities might exist to invite planners in particular to work within U.S. Army Futures Command or the Security Force Assistance Brigade and Security Force Assistance Commands. Such planners could help better integrate allied efforts in combined force planning, concept development, and engagement planning (see Chapter Four).
- **The Army should work with allies to ensure that embeds, exchanges and liaisons have clear, purposeful roles; identified and willing counterparts in each country; and senior leader support in home and host countries.** The United States and its highly capable allies could benefit from an across-the-board review of these roles and identification of new opportunities to bring allied military establishments closer together.

Allies Desire a Greater Role in Capability Codevelopment

The United States and its highly capable allies periodically collaborate on capability development, particularly in the design and application of new defense technologies. According to our allies, they would like to see more of these opportunities, especially in the science and technology space. Both Australian and British officials made the point that they would like the United States to share more information about capabilities and requirements-generation plans and processes as early on as possible. Knowing what new innovations are coming can help both sides determine if there are new codevelopment opportunities and inform allies' defense investments at home.

Allies argue that codevelopment provides them and the United States with force planning options from "inside the tent." Not every capability can or should be codeveloped, but allies' participation should be considered more routinely rather than defaulting to the Foreign Military Sales process. This includes identifying the appropriate allies for bilateral or multilateral codevelopment efforts. There are two key issues with using the Foreign Military Sales process as the default, according to capable allies. First, allies have little to no early-stage input, which leads to a certain level of ambiguity in terms of allies' national investments. If they invest in capability X, will it be compatible with technology Y coming from the United States? What about the details of technology Y? Are these details known to the ally? Second, many Australian officials shared their frustration with the slow, cumbersome Foreign Military Sales process, which often "spits out an exportable version of a technology for foreigners that is not interoperable with U.S. systems."[43] If allied inputs are not systematically incorporated in the early stages of the capability development requirements processes, interoperability problems are more likely to surface after capabilities are delivered. These challenges have been more acute for the U.S. Air Force, but the Army is not immune, particularly in the development of new technologies. Given the emphasis in the National Defense Strategy on interoperability with our

---

[43] Author interviews with senior Australian and British defense officials, 2019.

closest allies, early allied participation in capability development is a critical issue.

According to Australian officials, codevelopment of capabilities is about "being in the trenches together," with all participants investing their own resources in a venture and "experimenting and learning as they go."[44] From the perspective of U.S. allies, the more codevelopment opportunities in key capability areas, the better. Australia's strengths are intelligence, surveillance, and reconnaissance and early warning radar; the United Kingdom emphasizes submarine warfare, hypersonics, and network command, control, and communications. It is important to remember that U.S. allies have particular technology advances that the United States can learn from and potentially incorporate into its own capabilities.

Implications

The following two implications emerge from our findings on U.S.-allied codevelopment:

- **More-frequent early involvement of key allies in U.S. requirements- and capability-development processes is an important goal.** Codevelopment of military capabilities with the United States is an area of emphasis for highly capable allies. The United States should work with key allies to systematically evaluate options for codevelopment. The Army should consider inviting more active and substantive roles by key allies in the early stages of concept development, system development, and acquisition for systems that the Army deems necessary for effective interoperability. It should seek similar early involvement in allied initiatives as well (with full awareness of International Traffic in Arms Regulations restrictions and if classification challenges can be resolved). Such challenges could determine which allies would be appropriate for concept development (e.g., whether to limit concept development to Five Eyes countries). The new Army Futures Command might be in a position to facilitate some immediate opportunities. However, the Army will have to balance such opportunities for allied roles in codevelopment with the need to adjust its research and

---

[44] Author interview with senior Australian and British defense officials, 2019.

development processes to field capabilities more rapidly, effectively, and efficiently.

- **Further opportunities for collaboration in research, development, test, and evaluation efforts can benefit U.S.-allied interoperability.** As the United States focuses on multidomain operations, allies can serve as a valuable and synergistic source of new capability innovation. Working with highly capable allies on new capabilities might help mitigate the perceived tradeoff between interoperability and modernization.

U.S. Information-Sharing Restrictions Continue to Frustrate Allies

Although they are in place for good reasons, U.S. and DoD policies can block full interoperability with allies and partners. Information sharing restrictions are apparent through International Traffic in Arms Regulations and the liberal use of the "No Foreign Nationals" sharing information restriction by U.S. officials during deployments and for allied personnel in the United States occupying exchange and liaison positions. Allied individuals experiencing the restrictions in action highlight these issues with examples, particularly when they are unable to do their jobs effectively because they are not allowed to take part in a conversation or denied access to a certain critical document. This issue is also highlighted when allies are restricted from taking part in U.S. capability development, which—as emphasized earlier—ultimately affects interoperability. In addition, defaulting to restricting release of information to any foreign national (versus allowing release to Five Eyes countries) continues to hamper allies' full incorporation into the U.S. military planning process for major conflicts or other lesser contingencies. This remains a perennial challenge that determines the allies with which the United States shares sensitive information.

More broadly, allies stated that deliberate and crisis planning lags other areas of SC to support effective coalition operations. British and Australian respondents perceive that there is still some U.S. reluctance to relying on allied military power in plans for conflict against major adversaries. The U.S. culture emphasizes needing to prepare to "go it alone" out of uncertainty that coalition partners will participate in a contingency, and this culture might never fully disappear.

Implications

The following two implications emerge from our findings on information-sharing restrictions:

- **Review guidance on information sharing with key allies.** The Army should consider options for developing a more flexible form of classification guidance to more fully incorporate close allies into U.S. operations, planning, and concept development. At a minimum, it would be helpful for the Army to understand specific examples in which key allies have been unable to fully execute their duties, particularly as exchange officers, because of restrictions on releasability of information to foreign nationals and other International Traffic in Arms Regulations–related restrictions. Overall, we expect that this is an issue to be addressed at the levels of the Department of State and Office of the Secretary of Defense, not at the service level. The Army can explore whether there are Army process considerations that could mitigate constraints on information sharing regarding preferred communications systems and data repositories of information so that information could be releasable to staff from Five Eyes countries instead of not releasable to any foreign national.

- **The United States might find allies less prepared to contribute to coalition operations if they are not fully aware of U.S. operational plans.** In future contingencies, the United States might not be able to afford to go it alone; the United States will have to work with coalition partners to execute complex operations and potentially divide operational labor. In addition to addressing information sharing, the Army could also explore where there are opportunities to incorporate key allies more fully into planning processes—while acknowledging and taking into account concerns about classification, added risk of leaks, and potentially making planning processes more cumbersome. There also are likely to be differences between U.S. allies in terms of information that can be shared, even among allies like Germany, France, and Japan that are outside of the Five Eyes relationship.

Conclusions

In this chapter, we presented our most significant findings and implications related to operational partnering with highly capable allies by looking at lessons from recent operations in Iraq, Syria, and Afghanistan and seeking the perspectives of the United Kingdom and Australia on working with the United States and the Army on achieving greater interoperability in the future. Decades of working closely together as strong allies through combined training, education, exercises, exchanges, and other efforts enabled U.S. and allied forces to successfully conduct military operations together in the Middle East and Central Asia. However, more-systematic coordination, training, and sharing of information among allies in preparation for and during operations would have alleviated many gaps and inefficiencies. A review of how military relationships are implemented in terms of army-to-army talks, personnel exchanges, information sharing, and capability codevelopment is warranted; efforts to identify additional opportunities in these areas should also be made.

Security Cooperation with Highly Capable Allies for Engagement Partnering in Iraq, Afghanistan, and Beyond

In this chapter, we provide findings and implications related to the second area of SC with highly capable allies—engagement partnering—in the contexts of recent operations in Iraq, Syria, and Afghanistan and potential opportunities from the perspectives of the United Kingdom and Australia. We find that this type of SC with highly capable allies is conducted on a more *ad hoc* basis than in the case of operational partnering. There are opportunities to pursue engagement partnering with U.S. allies that would make related activities more systematic, efficient, and effective.

As with Chapter Three, the following sections are organized into findings and associated implications, with a brief presentation of supporting examples under each.

Security Cooperation for Engagement Partnering with Highly Capable Allies: Recent Operations

The findings in this section reflect SC for engagement partnering in current operations, which tend to include SC to

1. build local security force military capacity
2. improve capabilities for third parties to contribute to current coalition operations.

The expected benefits to the allies of sharing responsibilities for training and equipping local forces were recognized early in the operations in Afghanistan, Iraq, and Syria. The magnitude of the task of building national forces almost from scratch in Iraq and Afghanistan required the involvement of multiple coalition partners and itself demanded a carefully considered division of labor and coordination of effort. Engagement partnering—though expressed in other terms—was seen as part of an exit strategy that would allow coalition forces to transfer responsibility for domestic and national security to local forces over time and relieve foreign forces of security tasks so that they could eventually withdraw.

Training and equipping local forces was a long-term and central element to allied involvement in Iraq, Afghanistan, and Syria. However, partnering for engagement in planning, coordinating, and executing training of local forces was uneven and underdeveloped in Iraq and Afghanistan, where there have been both successes and challenges. Improving capabilities for third parties (e.g., ensuring less capable partners can operate as part of the coalition) to contribute to current coalition operations was an important activity in these operations, but presented fewer opportunities for learning lessons about engagement partnering. We touch briefly on training other coalition partners in our final finding of this section. We focus on coordinating SC for improving capabilities for other countries for future operations in the next section.

OEF/RSM (Afghanistan) and OIF (Iraq) were notable for their efforts to build local security forces from the ground up on a national level. They required development of land, air, maritime, and law enforcement forces and the institutional capacity to manage and sustain them across the board. Local forces needed to be trained to work and operate together on a national level and required coordination on approaches, organizational structures, and TTPs to enable cohesiveness when foreign trainers eventually departed. OIR (Iraq/Syria) was a much narrower initiative to train and equip local forces to pursue a particular mission—combating ISIS—limited in scope and time in threatened parts of Iraq and Syria; these forces would receive operational support from foreign forces (e.g., air support). There was much less of a requirement for similar training approaches or for disparate local forces to create similar TTPs so that they could ultimately work together. Iraqi and Syrian forces did, however, need to learn how to coordinate with coalition forces. Our assessment of engagement partnering in these operations leads us to different conclusions; engagement partnering in OIR seemed to lead to greater success than in OIF or OEF/RSM.

In the following sections, we present five key findings and supporting examples from our research into engagement partnering in recent operations and offer implications of these findings for the DoD and the Army. The first three focus on how the United States and its allies conducted their training of local security forces. The last two address broader strategic considerations for coordinating training efforts.

U.S.-Allied Efforts to Build Local Forces in Iraq and Afghanistan Lacked a Common Strategy

The United States and its allies lacked sound, agreed-upon strategies that would lead to a coordinated coalition approach to developing the capacity and capability of local Iraqi and Afghan security forces. We found little effort to develop a coordinated plan that laid out the goals and means that the United States and its allies would pursue and how they would measure success using a common framework. Not only was there an absence of a strategy for successfully building partner capacity, but the lack of coordination led to differing training standards for, assessments of, and approaches to local partners by the United States, the United Kingdom, Australia, and other allies.

This was particularly noticeable during OEF. For example, early in the conflict, the Germans took on the responsibility of training a new Afghan National Police force. Without coordination with other allies regarding standards, timelines, or budget, the German effort languished. Germany spent $89.7 million and trained 16,000 police, but their approach was not integrated with the rest of the coalition effort and resulted in the establishment of a three-year police academy. This academy had a curriculum that reflected German standards that were largely incompatible with the current situation in Afghanistan or with Afghan cultural norms.[1] Such lack of integration between allies was a hallmark of the first eight years of the Afghan mission, resulting in a series of setbacks and mismanaged expectations. In

[1] Judy Dempsey, "Germany Criticized for Its Training of Afghan Police," *New York Times*, October 15, 2006.

their haste to put in place functioning governing institutions in a devastated Afghanistan, NATO allies and the broader donor community neglected to develop a common vision of capacity building and to invest in the necessary coordination at the outset to ensure that their efforts were building toward a common goal.

The Special Inspector General for Afghanistan Reconstruction reinforced this finding in its June 2019 report:

> While the dual-hatted U.S.-NATO commander is largely responsible for reconstructing the Afghan National Defense and Security Forces (ANDSF), the Ministry of Defense (MOD), and the Ministry of Interior (MOI), the commander has no direct authority over civilian actors operating within embassies, the European Union, and other international organizations. Moreover, the commander does not have absolute authority to dictate the exact methods and activities NATO countries use to train and advise the ANDSF in different parts of Afghanistan. Rather the commander provides overarching guidance and coordinates the countries' various activities. This has created asymmetries in ANDSF development and has impeded the standardization of security sector assistance programs.[2]

Each NATO country developed its own approach to training, advising, and assisting the Afghan security forces and Ministries of Defense and Interior elements. The early days of OEF present examples of inadequate development of strategy and attention to coordinated outcomes. The Five Pillars of Defense concept, which emerged from an international conference in April 2002 on rebuilding in Afghanistan, was envisioned as a way for five willing countries to each reform a key area of the security sector: the army (United States), the police (Germany), counternarcotics (United Kingdom), disarmament, demobilization, and integration (Japan), and the justice sector (Italy). The Five Pillars concepts collapsed because there was

---

[2] Special Inspector General for Afghanistan Reconstruction, *Divided Responsibility: Lessons from U.S. Security Sector Assistance Efforts in Afghanistan*, Washington, D.C., June 2019, p. xiii.

no agreement on what being a "lead nation" meant and there was no strategy for how these pillars would develop together.[3]

This also was the case in Iraq, where there was no joint U.S.-British strategy for developing the Iraqi Security Forces. The United Kingdom ended up developing

> its own SSR [security sector reform] policies and plans for MND-SE [Multinational Division Southeast] without a clear understanding of how they contributed to—or whether they were fully consistent with— the SSR approach across Iraq.

The report continues, "It was unclear what success looked like and therefore how to measure it.[4]

In the absence of a common approach and in pursuit of fast transfer of authority to Iraqis, the focus of British SSR work "became the quantity of officers trained, not their quality . . . [T]here was a reluctance to pause and consider what was required to deliver the quality needed."[5]

In many ways, the difficulties that the United Kingdom faced mirrored those of the United States. The United States also began development of the ISAF in a whirlwind of confusion, with many fits and starts, and an emphasis on quantitative metrics because of the difficulties of assessing quality and the imperative to show progress. There also was a lack of agreement about what the Iraqi Army should ultimately look like.[6] Another area of disagreement was the use of U.S. and allied embeds in Iraqi units, with the United Kingdom deciding to forgo their use in MND-SE, depriving the United Kingdom of an ability to assess ISAF progress through close observation.

For all their coordination efforts on offensive operations, disparities in approach to training local forces were apparent between U.S. and Brit-

---

[3] See U.S. Government Accountability Office, *Afghanistan Security: Efforts to Establish Army and Police Have Made Progress, but Future Plans Need to Be Better Defined*, Washington, D.C., GAO-05-575, June 30, 2005.

[4] Chilcot, 2016, Vol. X, p. 440, paragraph 144.

[5] Chilcot, 2016, Vol. X, p. 440, paragraph 146.

[6] Author interviews with Australian defense officials in May 2019 and British defense officials in December 2019.

ish forces in Helmand, Afghanistan. According to one report, each nation formed adviser teams differently, and there was no unity of command among these teams. This lack of integration led to incidences of "'advisor fratricide' where multiple advisory efforts stressed different and sometimes conflicting priorities and outcomes."[7] Proximity and coordination also did not guarantee that lessons would be heeded. For instance, before Operation Moshtarak (which featured U.S. and British forces leading coordinated partnered operations with their Afghan counterparts), the British trained with the less experienced Afghan National Army, having learned that it was imperative to do so from previous experiences. However, the U.S. Marines elected not to train with the Afghan National Army; as a result, their operations in Marjah District did not go as well as hoped. In addition, the Afghan National Army brigade commander was embittered at not being involved in the planning.[8]

The absence of a preplanned, coordinated approach to building Iraqi and Afghan forces led to disjointed progress and resulted in some surprises when those forces were put to the test in operations. The most notable of these was the rapid disintegration of the 10th Iraqi Army Division during Operation Charge of the Knights in 2008 to retake Basra from Shia militia groups—after the division had been certified operationally ready. The lack of embedded advisers in this unit colored the assessment of the unit's readiness and deprived the Iraqis of the ability to call in air support and medical evacuation capabilities.

Implications

We identified two implications from our finding that efforts to build the capacity of Iraqi and Afghan security forces in OIF and OEF/RSM lacked a common strategy or approach:

- **Allied approaches to training local forces must be jointly planned and coordinated under an integrated strategy to ensure that they are aligned to both the objectives and scope of the training effort.** When the objective is to develop a national army from scratch, differing train-

---

[7] Powell, 2016, pp. 11–12.

[8] Farrell, 2017, p. 323.

ing standards and approaches to training local forces can create operational problems for those forces and make it more challenging for them to operate when they no longer benefit from allied support. Successful capacity building requires both a solid understanding of the desired end-state of the local force and a concept for how to get there in coordinated fashion. Moreover, as U.S. SC efforts increase focus on building the institutions of partners as well as military capacity, they can be more easily integrated with the traditional European emphasis on SSR.

- **Failure to establish a system of realistically assessing the operational effectiveness of local forces receiving allied training can lead to negative results when those forces conduct real-world missions.** Developing such a system should be a core element of planning for engagement partnering with allies. The Army is tracking ongoing DoD assessment, monitoring, and evaluation reforms, which could provide models for such assessments, and it is supporting efforts to develop capacity building and interoperability assessment approaches.

U.S.-Allied Coordination Improved Over Time with Some Notable Successes

Although there were challenges driven by the lack of a common allied strategy for building local forces in Iraq and Afghanistan, there were also some notable successes because of increased coordination for engagement partnering among the allies. In Afghanistan, better allied coordination followed the dissolution of the Five Pillar strategy and gradual adoption of more-integrated staffs charged with facilitating the training of both the Afghan National Army and Afghan National Police Forces. This was exemplified by the establishment of the NATO Training Mission–Afghanistan in 2009 and led the way for additional specialized schools and programs where U.S., Australian, and British forces often served together on multinational staffs.

As noted above, OIR—the coalition campaign to defeat ISIS—was a very different operation than OIF and OEF/RSM. It provides examples of successful engagement partnering with allies for enhancing local force capabilities through dedicated application of SC activities. The allies might not have had a common approach to training (which was not as important in this context as when building national security forces in OIF and OEF/RSM), but there was clearly coordination, and there was some evidence of operational success. In addition, coordination among the allies improved over time.[9] The United States, United Kingdom, and Australia divided areas and responsibilities for training Iraqi forces. Much of the training of Kurdish and Iraqi forces dedicated to the counter-ISIS effort was provided by U.S. allies, with the United States itself providing funding for equipment, infrastructure, and other required support.[10] In many cases, the United States funded infrastructure for training and developed programs of instruction, and allies conducted training. In late 2018, the United Kingdom coordinated with the United States in supporting five training bases for building local partner capacity in Iraq. The United Kingdom trained Kurdish Peshmerga forces and provided a niche capability for IED training that the United States did not have the capacity to provide. Similarly, Australia took the lead of a Special Operations Task Group that advised and assisted the Iraqi Counter-Terrorist Service during OIR. Australia also set up a logistics training center in Taji based on an Iraqi request, which filled an important niche that the United States was not filling. In the end, each ally (the United Kingdom, Australia, France, and the United States) managed one or more training centers dedicated to logistics, engineering, command and control, and combat operations.

Notably, allied trainers were able to get operational feedback on the effectiveness of the local personnel they were training and equipping. Some U.S. allies were prohibited by national caveats and established rules of engagement to conduct, advise, assist, and accompany missions with the units that they were training. A process was developed to consult with U.S. special operations forces that were authorized to accompany local Iraqi forces into battle. The U.S. special operations forces units systematically reported back to allied trainers on the effectiveness of Iraqi forces in the field in applying their training and the equipment that they had been provided, allowing allies to adjust their training regimens and approaches accordingly. This direct feedback was an important aspect of the success of the training program to counter ISIS.

---

9 "Operation Shader: All You Need To Know About Britain's Fight Against IS," 2021.

10 U.S. funding for such programs as the Counter-ISIS Train and Equip Fund did not cover the costs of U.S. forces' provision of training to local forces.

Implications

Efforts to conduct engagement partnering to train and equip local forces in the fight against ISIS in some ways provide an important contrast to the experience in OIF and OEF/RSM:

- As a corollary to the previous finding and implications, **the objectives and scope of an effort to train local forces can help dictate the extent to which, and at what level, allies need to jointly plan, coordinate, and execute third-country engagement**. Because of the well-defined mission in OIR—and the fact that the allies were providing critical components of the combat power (e.g., close air support, intelligence, surveillance, and reconnaissance, etc.)—Iraqi national, Peshmerga, and Syrian militia forces learned to operate together at the tactical level. Although it remained important that the allies develop an overall strategy for the training effort and divide labor, it was less important to coordinate approaches to training local forces.
- **Developing methods for assessing the operational effectiveness of local forces and sharing feedback with allies providing training are particularly important**. Observation of a partner in combat actively applying the training and operating the equipment that they had received is an ideal way of assessing the effectiveness of that training and whether the partner had truly absorbed it. When direct observation is not possible, allies should together seek alternative avenues of assessment and deriving lessons learned.

Political Imperatives at the National Level Shaped How Each Ally Approached Building Local Capacity

In efforts to forge an array of willing nations to support and participate in a coalition operation, the United States commonly expects the political leadership of those nations to impose national caveats; these caveats regulate the intent, scope, and limits of involvement of a nation's forces and set protocols for their actions in such an operation. National caveats are a very important means of eliciting the support of multiple nations toward common interests. They encourage inclusiveness by enabling countries to participate despite an unwillingness to conduct certain activities or missions. However, national caveats can cause surprises and challenges when operations are pursued in the field if there is not sufficient preparation to account for their limitations.

As highlighted in Chapter Three, the division of commands by geography in Iraq in the absence of a coalition strategy for stabilization and reconstruction allowed the development of discordant approaches across the coalition in their respective areas of operations. This extended to engagement partnering because of the existence of national caveats and disparate interests among the allies. The British, who took on an enormous responsibility for operations and training in an entire region (MND-SE), faced increasing domestic opposition to participation in OIF by the mid- to late-2000s, which in turn propelled an increasing aversion to casualties and a focus on two goals: force protection and withdrawal.[11] By 2008, with Operation Charge of the Knights, "British officials began to view the war as a political risk that needed to be minimized by limiting the British military's exposure."[12] This was the primary motivation behind the decision not to embed British advisers in the units of the 14th Iraqi Army Division that were supposed to provide security in the Basra area, thereby depriving the coalition of a way to assess the effectiveness of training and to help the Iraqis make appropriate adjustments to their concepts of operations.[13]

The experience of Australia with engagement partnering in Iraq was motivated by similar national caveats but resulted in a more acceptable outcome from Australia's perspective. Its involvement in Iraq was much less expansive than that of the United Kingdom, but it successfully scaled its contributions to building Iraqi forces to serve two national priorities: bolstering the U.S.-Australian alliance and managing U.S. expectations while minimizing risk and cost to Australia. Speaking about Australia's interest in demonstrating its value as an ally to the United States and its relative disinterest in Iraq, one interlocutor exclaimed: "Australia would have invaded

---

[11] Rayburn and Sobchak, 2019b, p. 381; and Chilcot, 2016, Executive Summary, p. 103.

[12] Maciejewski, 2013, p. 157.

[13] After the failures observed in the Iraqi Army's performance in Operation Charge of the Knights, British MND-SE commanders began embedding British advisors and military training teams into Iraqi units in Basra. See Rayburn and Sobchak, 2019b, p. 364; and T. G. S. Perkins, "Mitting in Basra During OP Telic 11—an OC's Perspective," *Royal Regiment of Scotland Journal*, March 2009, p. 36.

Antarctica if that's where the [United States] was going." In Iraq, "Australia's first priority was force-protection. Its second priority was force-protection. Its third priority was: see one and two."[14] The Australians agreed to participate in training on bases where there would be a lesser degree of risk. Australian personnel provided basic training to Iraqi Army recruits at the Basic Training Center at Tallil Air Base and served as counterinsurgency instructors in Taji; they also served at the aforementioned logistics training center at Taji during OIR.

Besides the political value of eliciting participation from multiple partners in a coalition, there is also operational value in recognizing the various national caveats allies and partners bring to a coalition and developing effective workarounds. In OIR, U.S. forces in Iraq were prohibited by congressional authorities from training Iraqi police. The Italian government specified that Italian forces were allowed to train police; therefore, the Italians provided a niche capability that could not be filled by the United States. Thus, Italian national caveats enabled the Combined Joint Task Force-OIR to work through a critical part of the plan, thereby strengthening the effectiveness of the Iraqi police.[15] Such caveats can in fact provide opportunities for coordination or can be leveraged to strengthen coalition engagement with partners.

Implication

A key implication for engagement partnering that emerges from the presence of national caveats is the following:

- **It is critical to consider how political imperatives will shape coalition approaches to developing local forces in third countries.** Effects of national caveats on capacity-building approaches need to be addressed explicitly when developing strategies and planning with allies for engagement partnering. National caveats will always be present; they encourage inclusiveness of coalition partners who have domestic political constraints but want to participate. The strategy for

---

[14] Author telephone interview with Australian academic, August 2019.

[15] U.S. Department of Defense Inspector General, *U.S. and Coalition Efforts to Train, Advise, Assist, and Equip the Iraqi Police Hold Force*, Washington, D.C., DODIG-2018-147, September 13, 2018.

coalition engagement must explicitly incorporate such caveats while making partner-building approaches as effective as possible. Understanding national caveats can help during planning to divide responsibilities among coalition partners, fill potential gaps, and improve coordination. Such caveats can be used in positive ways to the benefit of combined third-country engagement efforts.

Multitheater Demand for Constrained Allies Created Zero-Sum Allocation Problems

Because of their smaller size and limited resources, allies can be stretched thin by sizable commitments in multiple theaters of operation. This was the case with both the United Kingdom and Australia regarding participation in training efforts in both Iraq and Afghanistan as they were serving other priorities in regions of vital interest to them.

In the case of the United Kingdom, early in OIF and OEF, the British government began viewing Iraq and Afghanistan as zero-sum theaters that were competing for resources. The government quickly determined that the bulk of its effort should be reallocated from Iraq to Afghanistan, where it had concluded that a positive outcome was more likely. According to the Chilcot Report,

> [t]hroughout 2004 and 2005 it appears that senior members of the Armed Forces reached the view that little more would be achieved in MND-SE and that it would make more sense to concentrate military effort on Afghanistan where it might have greater effect. From July 2005 onwards, decisions in relation to resources for Iraq were made under the influence of the demands of the [British] effort in Afghanistan.[16]

By 2006, the British government had decided to withdraw its forces gradually from Iraq to increase significantly its troop presence in Afghanistan. This decision made deployments in Iraq and Afghanistan a zero-sum matter—the implications of which British policymakers apparently never discussed with their U.S. counterparts. This also influenced decisions in

---

[16] Chilcot, 2016, p. 99, para 721, Introduction, "Transition" section.

Iraq, where British trainers in MND-SE prematurely certified the 14th Iraqi Division operationally ready partly to hasten the drawdown in Iraq in favor of Afghanistan.[17]

In Australia's case, defense officials have lamented that the United States is simultaneously pressuring Australia to take a greater leadership role in its immediate region to counter Chinese influence and insisting that the Australian Defence Force stay engaged in ongoing operations in Iraq and Afghanistan (where Australia has been a valued partner in training local forces). At a strategic level, the message from the United States was for Australia to "dominate/control to the east and shape to the north" in its near abroad; at the operational level, U.S. commanders did not want to lose the Australian forces in the Middle East and Afghanistan. Many in the Australian Defence Force argue that manpower limitations from simultaneous contributions to operations in the Middle East and the Pacific are stretching Australia's forces thin and that Australia needs to direct its forces toward the most-immediate security concerns in its region, particularly with regard to contesting growing Chinese influence.[18] Strategy and policy discussions have noticeably changed over the past year to focusing on Australia's role in the Pacific and its new *Pacific Step-Up* initiative, which does not come with new resources for manpower but is rather a re-prioritization. Resources are flowing in that direction both in terms of economic aid but also in terms of security-related investments.

Implication

A key implication of this finding is the need for the United States to understand and openly interact with allies on the constraints affecting their engagement efforts, as follows:

- **Systematic understanding of allies' prioritization of global and regional commitments with allies is critical.** Despite allies' deep motivation to demonstrate that they are "with" the United States, the United States must be sensitive to allies' resource limitations and resulting allocation prioritizations and decisions. Both the United

---

[17] Rayburn and Sobchak, 2019b.

[18] Interviews with Australian and British defence officials, 2019.

States and its highly capable allies have common global interests, but allies also have key regional priorities (e.g., the United Kingdom in Africa, Australia in the Pacific). It is important that the United States and its allies have conversations around priorities that result in clear divisions of labor.

Some of the Most Effective Allied Training of Coalition Partners Took Advantage of Allies' Strengths and Existing Relationships

A key aspect of engagement partnering during recent operations in Iraq and Afghanistan involved training by the United States and its highly capable allies of less-capable partners to prepare to interoperate as a coalition in the field. The degree to which coordination occurs in operationally focused training with third party forces often depends on the importance of the training in achieving mission objectives. When training is critical to ongoing operations, more coordination takes place. Some of the most effective training appears to occur when responsibilities are distributed by geographic location and function to take advantage of allies' military strengths and political ties.

To support stability operations in Afghanistan, the United States invested heavily in training Central and Eastern European forces, building upon efforts begun in such countries as Georgia to develop counterterrorism capabilities and light infantry brigades through the Georgia Train and Equip program.[19] From 2010 to 2012, more than $285 million in global train-and-equip funding was dedicated to training ten countries for ISAF deployments.[20] The United Kingdom, focused on conducting training with such countries as Jordan (with which it has maintained a long-term security partnership) to improve their contributions to ISAF and enhance interoper-

---

[19] U.S. Department of State, "Georgia Train and Equip Program (GTEP)," press release, February 1, 2003; and Cory Welt, *Georgia: Background and U.S. Policy*, Washington, D.C.: Congressional Research Service, R45307, updated October 17, 2019.

[20] Nina M. Serafino, *Security Assistance Reform: "Section 1206" Background and Issues for Congress*, Washington, D.C.: Congressional Research Service, RS22855, December 8, 2014.

ability. A Jordanian contingent later deployed to Regional Command Southwest, where the majority of British forces were also deployed.

Finally, the aforementioned establishment of the NATO Special Operations Coordination Centre/NATO Special Operations Headquarters served as an important means of preparing coalition special operations forces for deployments to Afghanistan. This was the first coordinated effort to ensure that NATO allies and partners were training to the same basic standards and would be able to operate multilaterally and/or in contiguous battlespace. Nations with smaller and less experienced special operations capabilities were especially helped. Moreover, the centralized coursework conducted in Mons, Belgium was beneficial in building camaraderie across the alliance. In 2007, NATO established a Special Operations Coordination Center in Brussels to help coordinate training for forces from the Czech Republic, Estonia, and Poland to enable them to participate in ISAF. This center, which evolved into a NATO Special Operations Headquarters, continues to train approximately 1,000 students a year for coalition operations not only in the Middle East but Africa and Europe as well.

Implication

The experience with training partners to interoperate with U.S. and allied forces in Iraq and Afghanistan raises the following implication:

- **Division of labor among allies delivering SC to third countries works best when considering geography and allies' political ties and military strengths.** One of the "multiplier" effects of alliances is that bilateral relations between members of the alliance and other countries can benefit the alliance as a whole. Understanding where these allies have strong ties and the capabilities they can bring to bear would provide important benefits to coalitions. In areas where partners are primarily engaged in bilateral training, greater information sharing among the United States and its highly capable allies and transparency on these events could lead to more efficient preparation for both current and future multilateral coalition operations.

Security Cooperation for Engagement Partnering with Highly Capable Allies: Future Shaping

Engagement partnering for future shaping is about conducting and/or coordinating activities with highly capable allies to engage in SC with third countries to pursue strategic interests associated with long-term competition. Our findings draw more heavily on our interviews with U.S., British, and Australian stakeholders than on lessons learned from Iraq, Syria and Afghanistan, although some of the challenges during those operations do have bearing on engagement partnering going forward. Our analysis of lessons learned from recent operations and discussions with officials in Australia and the United Kingdom reveal opportunities for DoD and the Army to enhance the combined allied approach to engagement partnering in third countries in pursuit of combined interests.

We reached out to organizations in the Australian and British defense establishments, leading academics and think tanks, and key Army stakeholders to explore perspectives on existing and potential efforts to work together in third countries of mutual interest. We believe that the findings and implications here are likely applicable to U.S. SC for bilateral and multilateral engagement partnering with other highly capable allies, such as Canada, France, Germany, and Japan.

The findings in this section reflect SC for engagement partnering for future shaping, which have tended to include SC to

1. build partner capacity for future operations
2. gain access and influence
3. improve strategic competitiveness.

As discussed in Chapter Two, there could be many more opportunities for combined and/or coordinated SC among the United States, the United Kingdom, and Australia to meet these objectives.

The United States and Its Highly Capable Allies Bring Different Strengths to Engagements with Particular Third Countries

The United States and its allies all have different histories and current relationships with third countries—some of which might be apparent and obvious—but some of the nuances lie below the surface. It is important to attempt to understand these relationships and histories and acknowledge that the United States should not always try to take the lead. The United States and its key allies should understand the relative priority each accords to the third country, what has worked and not worked in the past and why, and any caveats and barriers to engagement.

Allies have different authorities by which they can engage partners, especially in a conflict. These authorities affect the ways in which allies train, equip, advise, enable and assist partner countries. The United States must understand those authorities and caveats at the outset of a collaboration and remain open to revisiting them as the political and operational situation changes. In turn, U.S. allies often have little understanding of the myriad authorities that govern U.S. SC and the limits that these authorities place on the types of activities that U.S. institutions (including DoD and the Department of State) can engage in, when, for how long, with whom, and within what scope. Combined planning is needed to identify opportunities for sensible collaboration and division of labor in third countries.

Institutional capacity building, or soft power, is one area that is potentially ripe for U.S.-allied collaboration and one in which allies might have advantages in particular countries. DoD has learned all too well that train-and-equip activities alone do not lead to sustainable capabilities in developing countries. U.S. allies have undergone similar revelations in recent years (for example, with Australia's Pacific Maritime Security Program and the United Kingdom's training efforts in East Africa). Partner countries often require a deeper level of support through institutional capacity-building efforts, which include reforming and modernizing such internal processes as human resource management systems, automated logistics systems, regulatory and legal processes, and concepts for developing new strategies and plans for a variety of missions. Planning with U.S. allies to support institutional capacity-building efforts or train-and-equip programs will also enable learning on all sides regarding each other's key strengths.

Learning more about allied strengths and weaknesses will also help identify allied authority-based thresholds and caveats. For example, the British Ministry of Defence maintains a medical caveat: It is unable to train partners to advanced medical standards because of liability reasons. Australia's international engagement program does not support robust infrastructure projects but rather is focused on training and professional education. The United States also has limitations on building new infrastructure overseas that is not intended to support U.S. military forces. Planning together will help to uncover more of the limitations and key strengths that allies bring to the table. Institutional capacity building is an area where the United States and its allies could explore collaboration opportunities for combining subject matter expertise to make partner countries more resilient, responsible, and modern. The trick is to ensure that the engagement with the partner is persistent and habitual in an effort to build trust, and that objectives and milestones are clearly understood by all parties.

Implications

We identified three implications of the finding that the United States and its allies bring different strengths to engagement with particular third countries:

- **At times it is more effective for allies to be in the lead rather than the United States given an ally's history with the partner and current relationship.** U.S. and allied proximity to a region, historical and existing relationships with third countries, and SC strengths should help determine roles each might play, including where it is sensible for a given ally to take the lead in particular engagement initiatives with the third countries.
- **The United States and allies will need to work to better understand each other's strengths and limitations in authorities and caveats in working with third countries through combined planning exercises.** This mutual understanding is better gained through interactions prior to engagements in the field. The effects of such limitations can create gaps and inefficiencies (such as duplication of effort) without working through such issues in a deliberate way during the planning process.

- **There are opportunities to work with key allies in institutional capacity building, which could include sharing insights into each other's engagement activities, planning together to achieve combined objectives in institutional capacity building, and coordinating key leader engagement talking points for combined strategic messaging purposes.** Our discussions with officials in the United Kingdom and Australia revealed that, among other areas of SC, institutional capacity building appeared to present multiple opportunities for combined planning and coordination of efforts.

The United States and Its Highly Capable Allies Need Much Greater Understanding of Each Other's Security Cooperation Approaches and Priorities

In addition to the issues identified above, our research has shown that there is a general lack of familiarization with the details and nuances of each other's SC organizations, priorities, planning processes, and resources. Typical conversations with allies regarding SC with third countries focus on filling (mostly U.S.) gaps rather than on truly investing in understanding and appreciating each other's SC structures and priority countries and regions (and broader national security objectives in interests that support these priorities).

Generally speaking, the United States has much more money and manpower for SC and a much more complicated SC enterprise focused on SC policy and strategy, planning, oversight, and execution. However, the United States is also more limited in terms of the rules that govern the use of resources attached to each SC program and initiative compared with U.S. allies. U.S. allies such as Australia and the United Kingdom are more centralized (at headquarters defense levels) in their approach to international engagement, have far fewer resources and programs, but they tend to have broader authorities attached to each program. In addition, some allies emphasize building long-term relations with partner countries through repeated deployments by the same advisors and trainers and long-term assignments over many years to enable deep cultural understanding and personal relationships in those countries.

It will take time and effort to learn about these nuances—more than just a briefing here and there—and key staffs on both sides should be tracking them. It is critical to understand each other's strengths and challenges— such as resource constraints and competing priorities, as in the case of Australia's prioritization of *Pacific Step-Up* over training efforts in Iraq and Afghanistan. The Pacific is a vital interest for Australia—where there is a widely held perception that inaction will lead to a loss of influence and access in the Pacific to China in a matter of years[21]—whereas the Middle East and Central Asia are not. The United States should become sensitive to such challenges through foundational dialogue with its closest allies.

Incorporating allies into U.S. SC planning is a good start, and the opportunity should also be made available for U.S. counterparts in the allies' defense structures. And it is important for both sides to not simply "share the final product" (a country plan, a new priority, initiative, etc.) but to consult during the building of the country plan or new SC initiative. It is also critical to involve allies in DoD assessment, monitoring and evaluation processes rather directly—the allies will likely provide valuable insights that will help DoD to better achieve its country and regional objectives, and they will be privy to best practices and lessons identified.

Our research has shown that the United States and its allies pursue common global objectives, particularly in terms of countering Russia and China's influence in key regions and countries. There might also be redundancies in U.S. and allied approaches—for example, where both the United States and key allies are selling platforms, training, technologies, and equipment to the same country. The closer the United States and its allies work together in the SC planning phases, the better these nuances will be understood and appreciated.

Implications

We identified two implications from the observation that the United States and its allies lack a nuanced understanding of each other's SC imperatives and approaches:

---

[21] Conversations with Australian and British defense officials, 2019.

- **The United States and its allies require discussions on first principles regarding political, military, and economic motives, priorities, and constraints.** As a first step in coordinating and integrating SC planning functions, U.S. and allied planners should enter into a structured dialogue to much more deeply understand each other's SC enterprises. Enhancing understanding across these enterprises would lay the necessary groundwork for defining combined SC approaches to regions and countries.
- **Take stock of current ongoing efforts with allies to work together in third countries and look for opportunities to focus them in a way that helps planners understand each other's SC approaches, processes, and priorities.** An important part of this dialogue must include experience from recent efforts to coordinate SC in countries such as Nigeria (United Kingdom) and Fiji (Australia). Case studies of these efforts could uncover examples of opportunities and challenges in working together toward common objectives.

Allies' Coordination with the United States on Third-Country Assistance Perceived as Tactical

From the perspective of allies, coordination of engagements outside Iraq, Syria, and Afghanistan has been *ad hoc*, reactive, and tactical. These allies have noted the lack of a coherent system by which to engage the DoD and the Army. Some areas of coordination are emerging in the Pacific and Africa, but these are more opportunistic and have not been institutionalized. Other initiatives have been more ambitious but have suffered from lack of resources and compressed timelines.

For example, there have been efforts in Europe to coordinate capacity-building efforts to strengthen NATO forces against Russian potential aggression. The TACET program was initiated in 2016 by Germany, the United States, and the United Kingdom to synchronize SC in Estonia, Latvia, Lithuania, and Poland. This initiative, which grew to include 16 countries, established 27 priority capability-development objectives for the Baltics and Poland to increase their interoperability with NATO. U.S. Army Europe took the lead in coordinating with allies to enhance training infrastructure, artillery capability, ground-based air defense, and intelligence and reconnaissance.[22] The program prioritized developing intelligence, surveillance, target acquisition, and reconnaissance capabilities and had some success in leveraging SC to improve intelligence-gathering capabilities in the region. However, the United States decided not to invest directly in TACET, which limited the utility of the program and its ability to achieve U.S. and NATO objectives.

After its initial two-year mandate, the TACET program evolved into a less formal Capability Enhancement Regional Symposium, which brought nations together to develop key capabilities. The Capability Enhancement Regional Symposium, which is administered by the European Command, lacks participation by some key nations, agreed-upon objectives, and reporting requirements, but it is able to target events at the NATO secret level to engage in operationally relevant discussions.[23] This includes forums on such important mission areas as maritime domain awareness and C4, which built upon previous intelligence, surveillance, target acquisition, and reconnaissance-related activities.[24] A TACET-like effort established in the Black Sea region to develop the military capabilities of Bulgaria and Romania, known as the Combined Joint Enhanced Training Initiative, also offered an opportunity to coordinate exercises and training but had a limited impact on leveraging NATO SC assets. It also failed to extend beyond a two-year period. Some thought was given to aligning U.S. train and equip initiatives to TACET and Combined Joint Enhanced Training capability objectives, but neither program received any direct U.S. investment.[25] The primary benefit of these programs was increased situational awareness of allied SC activities.

In addition, forums have been established to coordinate and deconflict allied SC activities, including the Multinational Working Group organized by the U.S. Indo-Pacific Command, and informal arrangements organized

---

[22] U.S. Army Europe Public Affairs, "U.S. Allies and Partners Work Together on TACET Initiative," U.S. Army, press release, February 10, 2016.

[23] Author e-mail exchange with senior U.S. defense official, February 27, 2020.

[24] Baltic Defence College, "EUCOM Capability Enhancement Regional Symposium," webpage, undated.

[25] U.S. European Command briefing, April 2017, Not available to the general public.

by U.S. Army Africa with the British Army. These information sharing sessions are important, but they do not take advantage of opportunities to do combined planning and execution in pursuit of common interests. There also has been SC coordination with allies at a country or tactical level, such as the coordination between the United States and United Kingdom on training and security assistance in Nigeria. This type of coordination has been more reactive to opportunities rather than proactively taking a strategic view through systematic combined planning efforts.

Despite these efforts, the allies continue to see the need for a more systematic approach to U.S.-allied coordination and integration of SC activities in important regions of mutual interest.[26]

Implications

Several implications emerge from the perspective that coordination between the United States and its allies on third-country assistance is *ad hoc*:

- **Emerging areas of subregional and country-level coordination should be more systematic and integrated.** There appears to be a need for a more formal framework for planning and coordinating combined U.S. and allied SC in third countries. Some of this could involve leveraging existing exchanges with highly capable allies. For example, the Army could consider expanding working groups in the ASTs with allies and include representatives from Army Service Component Commands to ensure synchronization with combatant commands theater campaign plans.
- **SC activities should be planned together, instead of simply making disjointed efforts to coordinate and deconflict activities.** Greater effort should be made to build upon regional SC initiatives to go beyond simply improving situational awareness to leverage allied SC assets. It would be extremely helpful for allies to actually plan together, including resourcing activities jointly, sequencing to maximize partner-nation absorptive potential, agreeing on Specific, Measurable, Achievable, Relevant/Results-Oriented, Time-Bound objectives, and using

---

[26] Multiple author interviews with senior Australian defense officials, May 2019, and senior British defense officials, December 2019.

assessment, monitoring and evaluation approaches to track progress and understand the outcomes of these combined engagements.

- **The United States and its allies should play to each of their strengths particularly when it comes to competing with Russia and China in gray zone countries.** The United States and its allies could focus on institutional capacity building, habitual engagements to build strong relationships, and combined support with a unified front toward common objectives.

A Framework for Security Cooperation Coordination with Third Countries is Needed at the Operational Level

Just as there is a lack of a systematic framework at the strategic level, there is no framework in place for allies to coordinate SC with each other in third countries at the operational level. There are some informal relationships, such as coordination by British 1st Division with U.S. Army Africa, and there have been centrally run clearinghouses and donor community efforts to coordinate assistance to countries and regions, but greater guidance and a framework at more senior Army ranks could be very helpful. For example, in the case of the United Kingdom, senior-level engagements, such as the GORTs at the three- and four-star level and the ASTs at the one- and two-star level, could include a focused discussion on SC with third countries. The GORT could identify priority regions and countries, and the staff talks could serve as follow-up and consider details at the working level. There could be a working group within the ASTs dedicated to deconflicting and eventually, synchronizing key third country SC efforts.

For this to be successful, U.S. and allied army officials should ensure that the relevant organizations attend the ASTs in particular. In the case of the U.S.-British ASTs, examples include U.S. Army Africa, 1st UK Division with its regionally aligned brigades, and the British 6th Division (in particular, the Special Infantry Battalion). For the U.S.-Australia ASTs, examples include U.S. Army Pacific, Australia's 1st Division (especially 3rd Battalion and 7th Battalion) and the Security Force Assistance Brigade (which is aligned to the Pacific). The Army National Guard State Partnership Program should also be included. These talks could also inform other efforts for synchronizing SC, such as the U.S.-Australia-New Zealand working group and general officer steering committee that guides combined engagement in Oceania.[27] Greater coordination would likely lead to greater congruence in training and standard operating procedures/TTPs in the field. The United Kingdom has even suggested embedding a British Army plans officer in the Security Force Assistance Command or the Security Force Assistance Brigade itself, though this could also be a personnel exchange. Establishing more direct connectivity between the regionally aligned brigades in the British 1st Division and the State Partnership Program would also be very useful, given the overlap in their missions, their approaches to SC, and overall agility. Neither require more than three to six months of lead time to plan and execute an engagement.

Implications

At least two implications emerge from the observation that a framework for engagement partnering at the operational level is lacking:

- **Planning and coordination among allied units would facilitate division of labor, development of common approaches to SC in third countries, and deconfliction at the operational level.** Encouraging frequent interaction among the key allied SC implementing units could enhance the effectiveness and efficiency of SC and ensure that allies become force multipliers to each other in pursuing common objectives in third countries. Such interactions could include U.S. and allied defense or army attachés and SC offices in those countries to ensure synchronization.
- **Engagement partnering might require a dedicated organizational construct to plan, coordinate, track, and assess combined U.S. and allied SC efforts.** This construct could be tested in the GORTs and ASTs to help link the strategic and operational levels.

---

[27] Written comment from senior Army official, October 1, 2020.

Conclusions

In this chapter, we sought to distill our most significant findings and implications related to engagement partnering with highly capable allies by looking at lessons from recent operations in Iraq, Syria, and Afghanistan and eliciting potential opportunities from the perspectives of the United Kingdom and Australia. Such coordination on combined SC efforts in third countries is more ad hoc, but opportunities to pursue engagement partnering with U.S. allies exist to make related activities more systematic, efficient, and effective. Such planning and coordination would enable the United States and its allies to present a united front in the effort to expand partner capacity and strengthen allied access and influence in the competition with Russia and China.

CHAPTER FIVE

Recommendations to the Army on Prioritizing Operational and Engagement Partnering with Allies

In this chapter, we present our conclusions and recommendations for the Army based on our exploration of SC for operational and engagement partnering with highly capable allies. The recommendations emphasize how the Army can apply the lessons of recent activities and the perspectives of key U.S. partners to its priorities in pursuing enterprise-wide SC plans. These are offered in the context of the ongoing HQDA initiative to develop an Army SC strategy, which we describe first.

Emerging Army Strategy for Security Cooperation

At the time that our research was completed, the Army is in the process of developing an *Army Strategy for Allies and Partners* intended to meet the priorities of the 2018 *National Defense Strategy* and support the *Army Campaign Plan 2019+*, a 15-year plan to integrate, synchronize, and direct Army actions based on DoD guidance and Army policy.[1] The *Army Strategy for Allies and Partners* and an associated implementation plan—termed Implementation of Security Cooperation with Allies and Partners (I-SCAP)—represent the servicewide institutionalization and operationalization of

---

[1] Office of the Deputy Chief of Staff, *Army Campaign Plan 2019+*, Washington, DC: Headquarters, Department of the Army, G-35/7, 2019, Not available to the general public.

this line of effort to integrate and synchronize SC across the Army. This new strategy is needed because of what has been a somewhat disjointed Army approach to SC that requires better alignment with DoD guidance, and a quickly evolving and increasingly complex and challenging strategic environment.

A strategic shift in U.S. defense strategy is underway—from a dispersed, regional focus on building partner military capacity against terrorist and insurgent groups to a more-centralized, global emphasis on interoperability with highly capable allies and strategic rivalry with near-peer competitors. Congress has mandated consolidation, prioritization, and evaluation of U.S. Government SC efforts under Title 10 (Chapter 16) and Title 22, prompting DoD and other U.S. agencies to develop synchronized planning, implementation, and assessment, monitoring and evaluation processes that take all interests, authorities, programs, and activities into account in holistic fashion. Emerging legal requirements add to the complexity, including expansive conventional arms transfer policies that address strategic competition and require targeted action plans and streamlined procedures for security assistance. The *Army Strategy for Allies and Partners* and the I-SCAP plan are being developed to respond to these evolving requirements.

The Army has been developing mechanisms that help institutionalize and prioritize the Army's efforts to strengthen U.S. alliances and partnerships—in particular, to establish more systematic engagement with highly capable allies such as the United Kingdom, Australia, France, Japan, Germany, and others. First, the Army has developed an Interoperability Campaign Plan, which defines the objectives and processes for enhancing interoperability with nominated partners and sets forth the development of interoperability roadmaps.[2] These roadmaps are developed and coordinated with the Army by partner planners in the Multinational Fusion Cell in the Army Staff. Second, the I-SCAP plan is intended to synchronize and integrate SC activities, including those identified in the Interoperability Campaign Plan, to attain the overall Army objectives and priorities set out in the *Army Strategy for Allies and Partners*. Third, the SC implementation plan will set forth an "All Things Allies and Partners" governance structure to adjudicate

---

[2]   U.S. Department of the Army, *U.S. Army Interoperability Campaign Plan 2019+*, Washington, D.C., 2019, Not available to the general public.

priorities and questions of resource allocation and, when necessary, tee up high-priority SC issues for Army leadership consideration and decision. The associated councils will be co-chaired by the Army Staff (Strategy, Plans and Policy Directorate [G-35]) and the Secretariat (Deputy Assistant Secretary for Defense Exports and Cooperation) to ensure that Title 10 and Title 22 requirements are considered in a holistic fashion.

The following recommendations are intended to inform the emerging SC implementation plan and "All Things Allies and Partners" governance structure.

Recommendations for Setting Army Security Cooperation Priorities in Operational Partnering

The first set of recommendations is derived from the findings and implications that emerged in our treatment of SC for operational partnering in recent and prospective operations. The Interoperability Campaign Plan and associated roadmaps go a long way toward setting forth a more systematic and coherent structure for planning and executing efforts to build bilateral interoperability with the Army's closest, most capable partners. However, we found areas in which enhancements could be considered.

Establish a Standing U.S.-Allied Land-Force Cell to Conceptualize, Exercise, and Execute Contingency Planning For Second- and Third-Tier Threats

The United States and its allies in NATO and the Pacific conduct deliberate planning on a regular basis to deter and counter first-tier threats in Europe and Asia. However, our survey of operations in Iraq and Afghanistan over the past ten to 15 years suggests that the allies did not conduct deliberate contingency or campaign planning as a means of jointly setting the strategic direction of operations—or changing that direction, as the case may be—and that the common approach was for the United Kingdom and other highly capable allies to fall in on existing operations (often led by the United States). In some ways, this would appear to be a reasonable approach to coalition operations with allies who have worked closely and frequently together for decades as members of established alliances. However, the absence of this type of joint campaign planning has led to misunderstandings over missions, objectives, operational strategy, implications of national caveats, and desired end states.

We recommend the establishment of a campaign planning cell manned by planners from the United States and its highly capable allies—not only the United Kingdom and Australia, but also Canada, France, and others—to be focused on lesser state and nonstate threats in regions where allies have strong interests in common with the United States. Existing organizational structures, including the Multinational Fusion Cell in HQDA and NATO Land Command in Norfolk, might already provide a framework for such campaign planning. Army Service Component Command planners should be involved to ensure that theater plans are addressed. The aim of the proposed joint planning cell would be to prepare contingency plans that lay out potential threats, coalition goals and end states, concepts of operation, roles and missions of coalition members (including examples of constraining national caveats), and potential command structures (including where allies might be in the lead). Gaps or challenges in contingency plan execution—such as interoperability challenges or missions for which an ally might need to prepare—could be identified and translated into SC requirements that partners or allies might be able to help address. For example, part of a campaign planning cell could bring the United Kingdom, France, and possibly Germany and Italy together to consider potential operations, missions, and roles in Africa were there to be a need for a rapid response to an emerging threat that required coalition response (e.g., combating a transnational terrorist group, humanitarian assistance). Similarly, planners from Australia, New Zealand, Japan, and Canada could join those from the United States in exploring potential contingencies in Southeast Asia or the Pacific Islands. Threats in the Middle East (including Iran) would certainly be a useful focus of a planning cell as well, involving U.S., British, and other allied planners with vital interests warranting their participation in a coalition. Problems identified could become objectives for SC between the allies or cooperative engagement in third countries.

The greatest challenge to establishing such a cell is the overclassification of U.S. strategic objectives and campaign plans that makes it difficult to conduct combined planning (an issue addressed below). There are potential costs associated with the activation of such a planning cell. Such exercises demand input from senior officials—who already might be taxed as they focus on current problems—and they run the risk of becoming unmoored from decisionmaking at the policy level. They also might inflame tensions between allies and partners when participants have very different perspectives on the national interests involved, the costs they are willing to pay, and their valuation of other allies' and partners' contributions. Finally, as more stakeholders become involved in planning, the risk of leaks to the media can increase. These challenges would need to be carefully considered and ameliorated before embarking on a systematic effort, but we contend that the potential benefits would be worthwhile and perpetuate a new kind of U.S.-allied military relationship.

In a sense, such contingency planning with allies could be considered a type of interoperability that is separable from the widely recognized human, procedural, and technical types. Just as traditional types of interoperability require systematic approaches and frequent engagement and exercises, a planning cell would facilitate the formulation and exercising of combined planning processes, expanded understanding of the capacity and willingness of the United States and its allies to form and participate in coalitions in particular situations, development of novel concepts of operation in advance of those operations, and the establishment of habitual and effective working relationships among planners.

Consider More-Formal Mechanisms for Predeployment Training in Future Contingencies Against Those Second- And Third-Tier Threats

As we discuss in earlier chapters and as borne out by G-TSCMIS data we accessed, little time was devoted to joint training between the United States and its highly capable allies during operations in Iraq and Afghanistan. There is no evidence that this significantly changed the outcomes of coalition operations—largely because of years of habitual U.S.-allied training and exercises and development of standards and TTPs under NATO and other alliances—but it did require devoting time and resources in the field to developing workarounds to challenges. Coalition forces could have been more operationally effective together earlier in their deployments had these workarounds been developed through predeployment, operational-level exercises. In the context of such potential contingencies as stability, peace enforcement, or counterterrorism operations, the Army and its components could consider engaging highly capable allies in conceptualizing processes for jointly spinning up forces rapidly prior to deployment in ways that account for specific operational environments and missions associated with a contingency, then measuring and improving baseline interoperability based on contingency requirements. When a contingency requires immediate response, little time might be available for such spin-up, and coalition forces would have to engage based on prior training and exercises. However, follow-on forces, if necessary, could be better prepared to deploy through such processes.

Identify and Incorporate Lessons Regarding Operational Partnering and Workarounds Into Exercise Planning with Highly Capable Allies

Recognizing that future coalition-executed contingency operations are likely to possess unique attributes that differ considerably from those of recent operations, there is very little evidence of follow-on efforts to maintain and internalize the interoperability that was gained there for application to future contingencies. ABCANZ has written some multinational doctrine based upon lessons, but there is little evidence that these lessons have found their way into U.S. doctrine, much less U.S. operational partnering approaches.[3] It remains important to capture more-generalizable operational and tactical lessons from the conflicts in Iraq and Afghanistan and apply them in U.S. exercises with highly capable allies. We identified several workarounds and innovations developed jointly by the United States and its allies to mitigate unforeseen challenges. These included changes in approach because of national caveats, amelioration of communications problems, and the creation of the Coalition Targeting Cell to ensure an integrated targeting capability. Although the specific characteristics of operations in Afghanistan and Iraq do not reflect the operational environments of potential future operations, such as near-peer conflicts, the identified gaps

---

[3]   Written comment from Army official, October 1, 2020.

in coalition workflow and adopted workarounds provide useful precedents for working effectively with highly capable allies in the future. Lessons from Iraq and Afghanistan on how to more effectively work with highly capable partners operationally need to be identified and prioritized for incorporation into U.S.-allied exercises. Such lessons could include those at the strategic level (the need to work toward a common strategy and division of labor appropriate to national interests and ally capabilities and caveats), the operational level (developing common operating pictures and logistics interoperability), and the tactical level (communications). The utility of bringing these lessons into exercises is to test their relative applicability in different circumstances and to ensure that they are not lost and then need to be reinvented in the field the next time there is a coalition contingency operation. The Army is already making inroads in this area through concepts associated with the Mission Partner Environment and should continue testing best practices in multinational exercises.

Seek Review of Classification Requirements to Enable More Inclusive Planning and Concept/System Development With Select Allies

Restricted releasability of classified information to allies is a perennial issue that extends both to operational planning as well as activities related to concept and system development. This issue is really in the purview of policymakers in OSD and the Joint Staff, but the Army can and should seek to initiate with OSD and the Joint Staff a review of classification requirements regarding information shared with its closest allies (starting with such partners as the United Kingdom, Australia, and Canada). The goal would be to enable more inclusive planning and concept and system development with select allies. A first step in this process would be to enumerate opportunities to forge new concepts that have been missed because of classification constraints.

Identify and Evaluate Additional Codevelopment Opportunities with Selected Allies

Developing a strategy for ensuring materiel interoperability and capability modernization is a key challenge facing the Army. The Army should identify and evaluate codevelopment opportunities in both the operational and materiel spaces, where selected highly capable allies can participate as full partners in the formulation of multidomain concepts to counter future operational challenges and to jointly pursue innovative initiatives in science and technology and development of system concepts. The allies that we engaged are very interested in expanding such opportunities. Moreover, some work on identifying codevelopment opportunities is already underway with the United Kingdom under the Modernization Collaboration Bilateral Planning Group and could be applied to other allies as well.

We find that allies often are not considered as partners upon internal initiation of concept or system development efforts in the Army or the other Services. This is strongly related to the previous recommendation on classification as well as differences in national priorities. But not considering allies at this early stage has two main effects. First, Army developers might inadvertently miss opportunities to benefit from innovations of U.S. allies. Second, interoperability might be more challenging to achieve after a concept or system is further along in the development and acquisition processes rather than having interoperability baked in from conception. Policy guidance might be required to ensure that new starts in concept or system development—or basic science and technology—formally and regularly balance rapid, effective, and efficient development of Army capability and system concepts with the participation of selected highly capable allies from the beginning of those activities.

Systematically Link General Officer Roundtables to Army-to-Army Staff Talks

Finally, GORTs are critical to setting and adjusting the direction of the army-to-army relationships with key allies. The guidance and taskings that emerge from these meetings should be addressed systematically in the ASTs and associated topic-focused working groups. Likewise, critical issues raised in the staff talks that require high-level adjudication could be addressed in the roundtables. This would help improve and sustain coherence and synchronization in plans to expand Army relationships with the armies of those allies. The Army should consider reviewing the goals of these meetings and their integration mechanisms with the aim of strengthening the links between them and making them more consistent. This would enhance planning for efforts aimed at operational partnering, including interoperability, and would also help set direction for engagement partnering, recommendations for which we now address. Some consideration is already being given to this under the U.S.-British relationship.[4]

Recommendations for Setting Army Security Cooperation Priorities in Engagement Partnering

The second set of recommendations is derived from the findings and implications that emerged in our treatment of SC for engagement partnering in recent operations and for future shaping. Unlike operational partnering, in which there are important but somewhat marginal improvements to be made given the long history of related alliance activities, SC for engagement partnering is a less well-developed area of U.S.-allied interaction regarding approaches to regions and partners of common interest.

Engage Highly Capable Allies Systematically on First Principles of Security Cooperation

In our interactions with both U.S. and allied interlocutors—and informed by some of our findings from building local forces in Iraq and Afghanistan—it became clear that the United States and its allies lack a complete understanding of the character and complexity of each other's SC enterprises. SC for engagement partnering with highly capable allies would benefit greatly from an effort to share first principles of SC with each other. An understanding of U.S. and allied similarities and differences in their approaches to SC, their perceived strengths and weaknesses, and policy and legal imperatives

---

[4] Written comment from Army official, October 1, 2020.

should precede any efforts to conduct combined planning and implementation of defense engagement with third countries.

Given its global, long-term outlook, HQDA is well-placed to serve as a motivator, coordinator, and integrator of such understandings. It can, both directly and via the Army Service Component Commands and the Army Security Cooperation Planners Course, make an effort to improve awareness of the SC approaches of key U.S. allies with third countries, and the U.S. side should devote to such discussions headquarters- and Army Service Component Command–level strategists, SC planners, regional foreign area officers, and others knowledgeable about U.S. SC authorities and processes, U.S. regional strategies, and U.S. priority countries. Questions to be addressed could include the following:

- What are their priority countries and regions and why?
- How are they organized and resourced for SC?
- What does their planning approach look like?
- What are their primary ways of engaging third countries?
- What are their strengths and challenges?
- What is their overall willingness to explore partnering opportunities with the United States?

It is not enough to presume that U.S. allies will be willing to fall in on U.S. SC approaches. Moreover, the U.S. allies have much smaller pools of SC resources from which to draw, and understanding where they seek to apply those resources is critical.

There is a need to find common objectives and complementary ways of engaging partner countries together. This would be a first step to understanding where systematic, coordinated engagement planning and execution might be feasible and equivalently beneficial to the United States and its allies, and where such coordination might not be advisable because of irreconcilable differences in priorities, interests, and approaches. Such efforts to understand first principles need not be limited to the United Kingdom and Australia; Canada, France, and other allies could take part on a bilateral or multilateral basis in sharing interests and approaches.

U.S. allies have expressed an interest in better understanding the complex ways the DoD plans, manages, and executes SC. They would need information on how the United States and the Army set SC priorities (and what those priorities are), how they approach planning, the role of the Geographic Combatant Commands and components, U.S. resource constraints and SC authorities, and how the United States conducts its assessment, monitoring and evaluation of its SC activities. For example, the Army could invest in efforts to better understand Australia's International Engagement portfolio (specifically the Defence Cooperation Program) while also taking time to explain the decentralized U.S. SC enterprise to the Australians. U.S. Army Pacific is already working with allies in the region through a series of working groups; such efforts could be considered for other regions as well.

Develop Global Security Cooperation Engagement Plans with Globally Engaged Highly Capable Allies

The Army service component commands are primary Army participants in planning land-force SC activities because of the centrality of the geographic combatant commands in SC planning and prioritization in their theaters. The Army service component commands are a key interlocutor with allies, and linking to geographic combatant command requirements and supporting them is paramount. The combatant commands are the primary synchronizers of SC in their theaters through their theater campaign plans.

As a military service, the Army also has an important role in guiding, planning, and implementing SC with allied armies and other external organizations in coordination with the Army service component commands. First, the Army must take a view of SC that exceeds the five-year time horizon of the combatant commands to support and implement DoD and Army guidance over the long term to develop capable land forces for future operations and operating environments. Second, as the United States' landpower service, the Army must take a global view that lashes together different geographic regions to meet global threats according to DoD's global campaign plan (upon which the theater plans are based). Third, the Army resources global requirements with funding, manpower, equipment, and basing, and must therefore plan, allocate, and evaluate those resources globally. Fourth, the Army must meet requirements of SC that might transcend the purview of the combatant command, including working globally with highly capable allies and meeting increasingly complex legal requirements, such as expansive conventional arms transfer policies that address strategic competition and industrial base issues that require targeted action plans and streamlined procedures for security assistance.

Given that the highly capable allies have interests in multiple theaters, the HQDA should serve as an integrator that would not only bring a global, cross-theater view of SC resource allocation but also a longer-term, service-level view of global land-power requirements. Such an integration role might require consideration of additional staffing and expertise in HQDA organizations that would adopt this role. Such planning efforts should be systematically implemented at both the strategic and operational levels and, in the case of the United States, in support of the DoD global and theater campaign plans. Figure 5.1 provides a schematic of development of combined engagement plans at the strategic level and combined execution plans at the operational level. At the strategic level, U.S. and allied planners at HQDA and the Army Service Component Commands would do the foundational work to define areas of overlap, duplication, and gaps in regions and countries of common interest and develop combined engagement plans that would define U.S. and allied roles and resources to coordinate SC in third countries over a year or more. At the operational level, implementers (potentially including components, the Security Force Assistance Brigade and Command, the National Guard State Partnership Program, country teams, and their allied equivalents) would plan and execute coordinated SC activities in particular third countries. These engagement and execution plans could be viewed as counterparts to the interoperability roadmaps on the operational partnering side of the house.

We do not offer this recommendation without acknowledging how challenging it could be to implement army-to-army planning and coordination of engagement partnering at the strategic or global level. One challenge is having ready access to the theater- and country-level details of SC that U.S. and allied planners at their headquarters might not normally have. Participation of—even co-leadership with—the Army service component commands is critical for this reason and to ensure fealty to theater campaign plans. A second challenge is navigating cases in which two or three allies have overlapping interests in a country or subregion, but one ally desires to initiate or continue cooperative activities there for its own interests even when it has comparative disadvantages vis-à-vis the other allies. Being

FIGURE 5.1

Strategic- and Operational-Level Engagement Planning with Highly Capable Allies

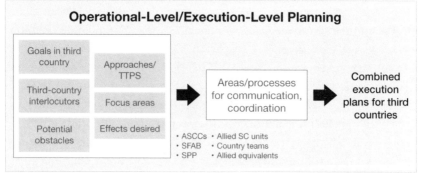

NOTE: ASCC = Army service component command; SFAB = Security Force Assistance Brigade; SPP = State Partnership Program.

aware of this in combined planning efforts would facilitate understanding of these interests and activities and aid deconfliction where possible.

Despite these challenges, we contend that the payoff of combined engagement planning and coordination would be significant. It would enable the United States and allied armies to understand each other's SC interests, constraints, strengths, and weaknesses at a global level; identify opportunities to work together toward common interests; and promote more-systematic coordination and deconfliction of activities. It could also help allies identify limitations, duplicative efforts, and gaps where activities could be rebalanced more efficiently through awareness of the SC resources that allies can bring to bear. Planning and coordination could also lead to development of common assessment, monitoring, and evaluation frameworks and means to collect and share information on progress in building third-country military and institutional capacity. Understanding globally where better coordination of resources and activities and division of labor are possible will help HQDA and the Army service component commands offer novel and more integrated ways of supporting theater campaign plans with the help of U.S. allies.

Conduct a Pilot Initiative to Plan, Coordinate, and Execute Third-Country Engagements with One or Two Highly Capable Allies

Building upon current U.S.-allied efforts to pursue engagements together in particular third countries (e.g., Nigeria), as well as the improved understanding of first principles suggested above, we recommend that the Army consider conducting a pilot initiative with one or two highly capable allies to conduct systematic combined planning, coordination, and execution of SC in regions and countries of mutual priority. The United Kingdom and Australia would be prime candidates for such a pilot. The effort could be threat- or regionally oriented and involving either or both allies and be limited in time (e.g., one year) and scope (e.g., against a specific mutual objective or in a single region or subregion).

We suggest establishing a centralized, service-level organizational construct, with its own battle rhythm, incorporating GORTs and staff talks, and including SC planners from the ally and HQDA and the Army service component commands. The construct would serve to identify areas where there is overlap and where there are gaps, where joint engagements in third countries could take place and with what SC tools, and where the United States or allies should lead combined efforts. This would help identify targets of opportunity to combine resources in support of common objectives, and to learn about the SC plans, priorities, and approaches of one another. The pilot could also result in combined engagement plans for countries and regions that integrate geographic combatant command and Army service component command country plans with those of the ally.

For example, a great place to start with Australia would likely be in the Pacific Islands; coordination between the United States and Australia in Oceania is already under way. The Army and Australian Defence Force could conduct an analytic tabletop exercise to identify capability gaps in engaging third countries in the Indo-Pacific. Then they could explore options to work together in the institutional capacity building and good governance spaces for strategic denial purposes vis-à-vis China and even augment each other's training and advisory teams with subject-matter experts from both the United States and Australia. This could involve developing synergies between the U.S. Pacific Pathways and Australian Pacific Step Up series. Together the two countries are very strong in this space and can work together to counter Chinese influence, particularly in the Indo-Pacific.

Planning and coordination in this pilot could also extend to the operational level and involve representatives from U.S. and allied execution organizations (such as the U.S. Security Force Assistance Brigade and Command and the British 1st Division). Considering that each of these units dedicated to SC are in their early stages of development, there is an opportunity to routinize some of the measures that have heretofore been more ad hoc at the broader service level. Following high-level decisions to coordinate execution in a third country, combined planning at the operational level could involve detailed understanding of objectives and tasks, focus areas for each unit and engagement, effects desired, approaches and TTPs, sharing of contacts of third-country interlocutors, plans and mechanisms for shared assessment, monitoring and evaluation, and potential obstacles to and mitigating responses for successful engagement.

Provide Guidance on SC For Engagement Partnering in The Army Security Cooperation Strategy and Implementation Plan

Both the *Army Strategy for Allies and Partners* and the associated I-SCAP should explicitly call out, institutionalize, and operationalize SC with highly capable allies for engagement partnering. It should be established as a priority that bolsters the U.S. and Army position in strategic competition and in posture. The implementation plan should frame how SC for engagement partnering could be applied with allies for institutional and operational capacity building in third countries. The plan could consider mirroring "All Things Allies and Partners" governance on the internal, institutional Army side with a small organizational structure with allies on the external, operational side. The organizational structure would involve G-35 and the Army service component commands (which would bring geographic combatant command requirements), Army security assistance professionals in the Secretariat (which would bring Title 22 and Conventional Arms Transfer requirements), and potentially Security Force Assistance Brigade and allied-equivalent leadership. Allied army representation could be included for issues involving discussion of Army SC priorities, planning, and assessment, monitoring, and evaluation in the internal "All Things Allies and Partners" structure; the U.S. could request representation in equivalent allied forums.

Conclusions

The Army's approach to working with its highly capable allies is evolving as a result of changes in national strategy and defense priorities, new DoD policies and processes, and an Army need and desire to forge a more holistic and systematic approach to its allies and partners. In this report we have sought to inform the Army's evolving approach with reflections on recent operations and the perspectives of key allies on operational and engagement partnering, and to provide practical recommendations for finding opportunities to work more closely together toward common interests. Our treatment of partnering incorporated interoperability—a key objective—but went well beyond it to consider potentially fruitful areas of strategic-level planning and coordination with U.S. allies. More systematic partnering will extend the competitive advantage alliances and partnerships offer to the United States vis-à-vis its rivals.

Addendum: The Impact of the Coronavirus Disease 2019 Pandemic on Security Cooperation

After the research for this report was completed, COVID-19 brought most bilateral and multilateral activities planned by the United States and its allies—including Australia and the United Kingdom—to a grinding halt.

With regards to Australia, key exercises, including the capstone Royal Australian Air Force multinational Pitch Black, were canceled; other exercises, such as Talisman Sabre (Joint) and Hamel (Australian Army), might be rescheduled, reconfigured to virtual events, or canceled. The United States can no longer engage with its highly capable allies in many traditional ways, but it still needs to maintain contact and operational readiness.

Preliminary RAND work on the national security effects of COVID-19 suggests that the United States and the Army will need to adjust to these challenges and look for new opportunities to strengthen SC with key allies and partners. It appears that the pandemic will ebb and flow in different countries and regions; at the time of writing, COVID-19 was less controlled in the United States than in some of its allies. SC activities might resume, at least in limited fashion, in places where there is already U.S. presence; in some cases, it might be more challenging to engage in person when intercontinental travel is needed, and SC events may be virtual, postponed, or canceled. In the longer term, it is less clear how this experience will affect U.S. SC efforts to address strategic challenges. The effects of the pandemic are likely to be significant for all U.S. allies and partners.

However, the crisis perhaps provides a unique opportunity to rethink how to work with key allies to engage each other and third countries. DoD would be wise to develop country-specific courses of action to mitigate these impacts against a variety of possible COVID-19 scenarios. The United States and its key allies could consider using this COVID-19–driven hiatus to engage in some out-of-the-box collaborative planning. For example, as recommended above, there is likely to be scope to launch a pilot case to develop one combined SC plan for engaging one or two partner countries. In working with third countries in the Indo-Pacific, the United States should consider working more collaboratively with Australia to support the Pacific Step Up, facilitating Australian on-the-ground activities with such enablers as logistics, transportation, intelligence, surveillance, and engineering support. Such combined efforts could be planned virtually in the near term.

Research Approach

We adopted a mixed-method approach to this study, combining a literature review of previous findings on SC uses and effectiveness, a database analysis of recent U.S. SC, a historical analysis of secondary sources documenting recent overseas contingency operations, and interviews with key stakeholders in the United States, the United Kingdom, and Australia.

This appendix discusses the assumptions and caveats underpinning our research approach, summarizes our analysis of SC events with allies through the G-TSCMIS database as well as our exploration of lessons learned databases, identifies key sources for our historical analysis of operations in Iraq and Afghanistan, and offers our protocol for interviews with key Australian and British stakeholders.

Assumptions and Caveats

This approach reflects a "wide net" strategy to pull as much information in as possible to identify lessons for prioritizing ongoing and future SC with highly capable allies. This strategy rests on the following assumptions:

- A retrospective analysis of SC activities provides a useful roadmap for future activities.
- Lessons from operations in Iraq, Syria, and Afghanistan are sufficiently generalizable to develop understanding for possible near-peer operations.
- Lessons from the United Kingdom and Australia will be useful for other highly capable allies.

We believe each of these assumptions is warranted for this analysis. The lessons from our empirical analyses of operations in Iraq, Syria, and Afghanistan and of the broader set of activities included in the database of recent U.S. SC match with considerations that U.S., British, and Australian stakeholders recognized as important for future SC initiatives. Operations in Iraq, Syria and Afghanistan are different than the potential near-peer conflicts that the United States and its highly capable allies are preparing for, but we expect the operational aspects of coalition partnering are generalizable from Iraq, Syria, and Afghanistan to future coalition operations. Finally, U.S. SC with the United Kingdom and Australia is more intense than with most other highly capable allies. This SC might not be representative of all SC, but (1) it represents two important partnerships that the Army is currently working to further institutionalize and (2) we expect the constraints on SC felt between these three countries are likely to be more binding for other countries, such as Canada, France, and Germany. Resource constraints prevented us from doing in-depth analyses of other highly capable allies; we include Canada, France, Germany, and Italy in our G-TSCMIS analysis to assess whether patterns in SC between the United States and its other highly capable allies looks significantly different than with the United Kingdom and Australia.

There are some caveats to this process. First, the Army and DoD are changing their SC processes. The greater the changes, the less applicable the findings in this report might be. Second, the greater the difference in planning and execution of future operations to the planning and execution of operations in Iraq, Syria, and Afghanistan, the less relevant the results from this study will be for prioritizing SC with highly capable allies. Third, as the United States, the United Kingdom, and Australia take steps to further institutionalize their SC planning, these relationships might become less useful exemplars for SC with other highly capable allies.

Global Theater Security Cooperation Management Information System

We conducted an analysis of the U.S. SC engagements that were recorded in G-TSCMIS. G-TSCMIS is a collaborative tool used by the global combatant commands to track SC activities across the globe. Although not all DoD activities are recorded in G-TSCMIS, it remains the most comprehensive listing of global SC engagements and the system of record for DOD SC reporting requirements. G-TSCMIS suffers from variability in its data reporting across time and reporting organizations, but no other resource provides a better overview of the nature and frequency of U.S. SC activities with highly capable allies. As we relied on G-TSCMIS to identify representative examples of U.S. SC, not the distribution of all U.S. SC, we believe that the limitations of G-TSCMIS as a data repository do not jeopardize this analysis.

Our research approach consisted of downloading all completed SC events included in G-TSCMIS that involved at least one of the following U.S. highly capable allies: Australia, Canada, France, Germany, Italy, and the United Kingdom. It is important to note that although our in-depth analyses focused on the United Kingdom and Australia, we include Canada, France, Germany and Italy in this analysis to develop a broader understanding of U.S. SC activities with highly capable allies.

We captured all events within the widest possible timeframe, pulling all available data during fiscal years 2002 to 2018. As many of the events involved more than one partner, we deleted all duplicate events. Most G-TSCMIS event entries are unclassified; we excluded a small number of classified entries and focused on the 8,153 unique unclassified SC activities between the United States and at least one of the six identified highly capable allies that occurred from fiscal years 2002 through 2018.

Many of these activities were multinational events. These events were then binned by type (*SC tool*). The most common SC tools in G-TSCMIS were defense and military contacts; combined/multinational exercises; combined/multinational education; and combined multinational training. Other SC tools that the U.S. military used to engage with partners included counternarcotics assistance; humanitarian assistance; information sharing/intelligence cooperation; and operations. Approximately half of the events that occurred with the selected partners were defense and military contacts. Examples of defense and military contracts include leader staff talks, regional working groups, calls between defense attachés, and ABCANZ meetings. Defense and military contacts were the most frequently used SC tool for U.S. engagement with each ally, followed by exercises. Beginning in fiscal year 2016, SC activities entered into G-TSCMIS can be tagged with an event purpose. The most common event purpose for the events in the selected period with these allies was interoperability. "Other," maritime security, and coalition operations were the next most common event purposes. Of the 8,153 SC activities with the six highly capable allies, fewer than 100 related to activities in Iraq and Afghanistan; almost none of the excluded classified entries referred to Iraq, Syria, or Afghanistan.

Analysis of Lessons Learned

We also did a search of all lessons learned literature available on recent operations in Afghanistan and Iraq. This included an extensive search of the Joint Lessons Learned Information System database, which includes a variety of observations and reports written over the course of 20 years. These include operational and exercise reports, DoD inspector general reports to Congress, and decades of war analyses. We also looked at allied reporting, including reports to the British House of Commons on operations in Iraq.

Historical Analyses

The following sections list the sources on which our historical analyses were based:

Key Works for Iraq

- British Army, Office of the Chief of the General Staff, *Stability Operations in Iraq (OP TELIC 2-5): An Analysis from a Land Perspective*, London, Army Code 71844, 2006.
- British Ministry of Defence, *Delivering Security in a Changing World: Future Capabilities*, London, white paper, July 2004.
- Carney, Stephen A., *Allied Participation in Operation Iraqi Freedom*, Washington, D.C.: Center for Military History, United States Army, 2011.

- Chilcot, John, *The Report of the Iraq Inquiry*, London: National Archives, July 6, 2016.
- Maciejewski, Justin, "'Best Effort': Operation Sinbad and the Iraq Campaign," in Jonathan Bailey, Richard Iron, and Hew Strachan, eds., *British Generals in Blair's Wars*, Surrey, United Kingdom: Ashgate Publishing, 2013, pp. 157–174.
- Palazzo, Albert, *The Australian Army and the War in Iraq: 2002–2010*, Canberra: Australian Army, March 2011.
- Rayburn, Joel D., and Frank K. Sobchak, eds., *The U.S. Army in the Iraq War, Volume 1: Invasion, Insurgency, Civil War, 2003–2006*, Carlisle, Pa.: Strategic Studies Institute and U.S. Army War College Press, January 2019a.
- Rayburn, Joel D., and Frank K. Sobchak, eds., *The U.S. Army in the Iraq War, Volume 2: Surge and Withdrawal, 2007–2011*, Carlisle, Pa.: Strategic Studies Institute and U.S. Army War College Press, January 2019b.
- Ripley, Tim, *Operation Telic: The British Campaign in Iraq in 2003–2009*, Lancaster, United Kingdom: Telic-Herrick Publications, 2014.
- Sky, Emma, *The Unravelling: High Hopes and Missed Opportunities in Iraq*, New York: Public Affairs, 2015.

Key Works for Afghanistan

- British Army, *Operation HERRICK Campaign Study*, Warminster, March 2015.
- Brooke-Holland, Louisa, *Troops in Afghanistan: July 2018 Update*, United Kingdom House of Commons Library, Briefing Paper Number 08292, July 13, 2018.
- Egnell, Robert, "Lesson from Helmand, Afghanistan: What Now for British Counterinsurgency?" *International Affairs (Royal Institute of International Affairs, 1944–)*, Vol. 87, No. 2, March 2011, pp. 297–315.
- Farrell, Theo, "Improving in War: Military Adaptation and the British in Helmand Province, Afghanistan, 2006–2009," *Journal of Strategic Studies*, Vol. 33, No. 4, 2010, pp. 567–594.
- Farrell, Theo, *Unwinnable: Britain's War in Afghanistan, 2001–2014*, London: Bodley Head, 2017.

- Feike, Markus, "German Experiences in Police Building in Afghanistan," National Graduate Institute for Policy Studies, Discussion Paper 10-02, 2010.
- King, Matt, *1st (United Kingdom) Division Capacity Building Overview*, briefing, January 23, 2019.
- Morelli, Vincent, and Paul Belkin, *NATO in Afghanistan: A Test of the Transatlantic Alliance*, Washington, D.C.: Congressional Research Service, RL33627, December 3, 2009.
- Powell, Alexander, Larry Lewis, Catherine Norman, and Jerry Meyerle, *Summary Report: U.S.-UK Integration in Helmand*, Arlington, Va.: Center for Naval Analysis, February 2016.
- "RUSI Interview with General David Richards," *RUSI Journal*, Vol. 152, No. 2, 2007, pp. 24–33.
- United Kingdom Army Directorate Land Warfare, *Preparing for Transition in Afghanistan*, briefing, 2010.

Interviews with U.S., British, and Australian Officials

We conducted discussions with U.S., British, and Australian officials both in the United States and during field visits to the United Kingdom and Australia. Table A.1 provides a list of organizations with which we conducted discussions and the numbers of discussions we conducted. To understand British and Australian perspectives on improving SC with the United States, we interviewed senior Australian and British defense officials at the Policy, Service headquarters, and unit levels, including those with direct knowledge of how Australia and the United Kingdom supported coalition operations in Iraq and Afghanistan. We also elicited written feedback on an early draft of this report from several Army organizations.

TABLE A.1

Organizations Engaged to Support This Research

Organization	Number of Senior-Level Participants
U.S. organizations	
HQDA/Stability and Security Cooperation Division (DAMO-SSC) (multiple discussions)	3
HQDA/Army International Affairs Division (DAMO-SSR)	3
U.S. Embassy (Canberra, Australia)	2
Deputy Assistant Secretary of the Army for Defense Exports and Cooperation (DASA-DE&C)	1
U.S. Army Training and Doctrine Command	1
U.S. Army Forces Command	1
I Corps	1
U.S. Army Pacific	1
Peacekeeping and Stability Operations Institute	1
British organizations	
Ministry of Defence/Security Policy and Operations: Military Strategy	3
Army International Branch	2
Land Operations Command	3
1st Division	2
3rd Division	3
6th Division	3
British Embassy (Washington, D.C.)	3
Royal United Services Institute	1
Australian organizations	
Department of Defence/Strategic Policy Division	3
Department of Defence/International Policy Division	9
Joint Operations Command	3

Table A.1—continued

Organization	Number of Senior-Level Participants
Department of Defence/Capability Acquisition and Sustainment Group	1
Australian Army Staff	6
Australian Single Services (other)	6
Department of Foreign Affairs and Trade	1
Office of National Intelligence	1
Australian National University	3
Australian Strategic Policy Institute	3
Australian Embassy (Washington, D.C.)	2

The questionnaire below is the interview protocol that we used to engage with officials in the British security establishment; it is representative of the questions posed to Australian counterparts and to other subject-matter experts in Australia, the United Kingdom, and the United States. The term *high-end* is used interchangeably with *highly capable*.

Prioritizing Army SC—Interview Questions for UK Interviews

Study Background

RAND's Arroyo Center is conducting a study for the U.S. Army Staff that seeks to help the Army understand how to prioritize defence engagement (UK term akin to security cooperation) with high-end U.S. allies.

We think about defence engagement with high-end allies as planning, coordination, and preparation for two different sets of combined efforts: (1) commanding, controlling, and operating together in conflict; and (2) building local capacity and allied influence in 3rd countries based on common interests.

Our approach is both operationally- and ally-focused. Because of our scope, we are looking at operations in Iraq/Syria and Afghanistan to understand the recent scope of such engagement. And we are reaching out to British and Australian experts to understand allied perspectives on these operations and on future opportunities for defence engagement.

We appreciate your taking the time to speak with us. Your input will be critical to the framing of our analysis. We will be taking detailed notes during this interview, but your responses will be kept anonymous; we will not share our interview notes or your personal information outside our project team. And of course, if you don't feel comfortable answering any of these questions, please just let us know.

Do you have any questions before we begin our interview?

Interviewee Background
- What is your current position?
- Could you describe positions you've had related to working with the U.S. military or DoD?
- Are you now or have you been involved in defence engagement? With the U.S. or with other allies, or in planning/resourcing? In what capacity?

[Select questions based on interviewee's experience/positions]

Iraq/Syria/Afghanistan
- What were the UK's national priorities in [Iraq/Syria/Afghanistan]?
  - What constraints did UK leadership place on participation in the operations?
  - How did these priorities and constraints impact the UK's role in these operations?
  - How did these priorities and constraints impact UK interactions with its coalition allies, especially the U.S.?

Engagement in preparation for combat operations in Iraq/Syria/Afghanistan
- What were/are the UK's operational roles in the conflict in which you were involved?
- What examples of UK-U.S. predeployment/employment engagement can you cite that were designed to plan, coordinate, and otherwise prepare for combined operations in [Iraq/Syria/Afghanistan]?

- – If examples can be cited, what were the operational effects of such engagements and preparations?
- – If examples cannot be cited, were there observable negative effects on combined operations, or can you discern any effects from the absence of such examples?
- What lessons emerge from operations in [Iraq/Syria/Afghanistan] for UK-U.S. engagement to prepare for future coalition operations?
  - – What mechanisms should the UK and U.S. use to ensure that the lessons are internalized and applied?

Engagement in preparation for and implementation of train/equip/advise/ assist local Iraqi/Syrian/Afghan security forces
- What were/are the roles the UK played/plays in training/equipping/ advising/assisting [Iraqi/Syrian/Afghan] security forces?
  - – What were roles where the UK took the lead or provided particular niche capability and training?
- What examples of UK-U.S. engagement can you cite that were designed to plan, coordinate, and otherwise prepare for building the capacity of local security forces in [Iraq/Syria/Afghanistan]?
  - – If examples can be cited, what were the effects of such engagements and preparations?
  - – If examples cannot be cited, were there observable negative effects on the ability to build local security forces, or can you discern any effects from the absence of such examples?
- What lessons emerge from train/equip/advise/assist efforts in [Iraq/ Syria/Afghanistan] for UK-U.S. engagement to coordinate the building of capacity and influence in 3rd countries?
  - – What mechanisms should the UK and U.S. use to ensure that the lessons are internalized and applied?

Emerging/Future Opportunities
Engagement in preparation for combat operations
- What are the UK's deterrence and defence priorities around the world?
  - – Which regions, which countries?
  - – For what objectives?

- Where are the UK and U.S. working together to build interoperability and common defenses?
  - Where do you think each has particular strengths or weaknesses?
  - What mechanisms are being used to work with the U.S. in general and U.S. Army in particular? Who (or what organizations) do you work with on the U.S. side?
  - What constraints are there to doing this successfully?
- What improvements would you like to see in UK-U.S. engagement to prepare for future coalition operations?
  - Why are these improvements needed?
  - What types of UK-U.S. engagement in this realm would you like to see the U.S. prioritize?
    - Exercises?
    - Codevelopment of concepts and systems?
  - What mechanisms should be used to plan and implement such UK-U.S. engagement?
    - Key leader engagements?
    - Staff talks?
    - Personnel exchanges or [liaison officers]?

Engagement in preparation for and implementation of activities in 3rd countries
- What are the UK's defense engagement priorities around the world?
  - Which regions, which countries?
  - For what objectives?
- Where are the UK and U.S. working together to build capacity of 3rd countries and allied influence in those countries?
  - What mechanisms are being used to work with the U.S. in general and U.S. Army in particular? Who (or what organizations) do you work with on the U.S. side?
  - Where would coordination efforts be most valuable to the UK?
  - What constraints are there to doing this successfully?
- What improvements would you like to see in UK-U.S. engagement to coordinate security cooperation in 3rd countries in pursuit of common UK-U.S. interests?
  - Why are these improvements needed?

- What types of UK-U.S. engagement in this realm would you like to see the U.S. prioritize?
  - Notification only?
  - Deconfliction?
  - Coordination/implementation of events in 3rd countries?
  - Strategic planning/coordination of 3rd-country and regional approaches?
- What mechanisms should be used to plan and implement such UK-U.S. engagement?
  - Key leader engagements?
  - Staff talks?
  - Personnel exchanges or [liaison officers]?
  - Planning conferences?
  - Coordination between Special Infantry Group and Security Force Assistance Brigade?

Additional Information
- Are there other experts with whom you'd recommend that we talk to regarding any of the topics we have covered today?
- Are there any documents that you would recommend we review? E.g., those that refer to preparations for combined operations and training of local forces in Iraq, Syria, and Afghanistan? Those that outline where the UK and U.S. are/should be coordinating on engagement with 3rd countries now and in the future?

Abbreviations

ABCANZ	American, British, Canadian, Australian and New Zealand Armies Program
AST	Army Staff Talk
COVID-19	coronavirus disease 2019
DoD	U.S. Department of Defense
G-35	Strategy, Plans and Policy Directorate
GORT	General Officer Roundtable
G-TSCMIS	Global Theater Security Cooperation Management Information System
HQDA	Headquarters, Department of the Army
IED	improvised explosive device
ISAF	International Security Assistance Force
I-SCAP	Implementation of Security Cooperation with Allies and Partners
ISIS	Islamic State of Iraq and Syria
MND-SE	Multinational Division Southeast
NATO	North Atlantic Treaty Organization
OEF	Operation Enduring Freedom
OIF	Operation Iraqi Freedom
OIR	Operation Inherent Resolve
RSM	Resolute Support Mission
SC	security cooperation
SSR	security sector reform
TACET	Transatlantic Capability Enhancement and Training Initiative
TTPs	tactics, techniques, and procedures

Bibliography

Allen, James, "Soldiers in Africa Get French Commando Training," U.S. Army, press release, February 9, 2007. As of July 13, 2021:
https://www.army.mil/article/1777/
soldiers_in_africa_get_french_commando_training

Australian Government Department of Defence, *2016 Defence White Paper*, Canberra, 2016. As of July 13, 2021:
https://www.defence.gov.au/whitepaper/Docs/2016-Defence-White-Paper.pdf

Baltic Defence College, "EUCOM Capability Enhancement Regional Symposium," webpage, undated. As of February 27, 2020:
http://www.baltdefcol.org/?id=1499

Beaton, Michael, "Unified Endeavor 14-01 Prepares U.S./Multinational Soldiers for ISAF Deployment," U.S. Army, webpage, October 16, 2013. As of February 25, 2020:
https://www.army.mil/article/113201/unified_endeavor_14_01_prepares_
usmultinational_soldiers_for_isaf_deployment

British Army, Office of the Chief of the General Staff, *Stability Operations in Iraq (OP TELIC 2-5): An Analysis from a Land Perspective*, London, Army Code 71844, 2006.

British Army, *Operation HERRICK Campaign Study*, Warminster, March 2015. As of July 13, 2021:
https://assets.publishing.service.gov.uk/government/uploads/system/uploads/
attachment_data/file/492757/20160107115638.pdf

British Ministry of Defence, Delivering Security in a Changing World: Future Capabilities, London, white paper, July 2004.

Brooke-Holland, Louisa, *Troops in Afghanistan: July 2018 Update*, United Kingdom House of Commons Library, Briefing Paper Number 08292, July 13, 2018.

Brooks, Drew, "U.S., U.K. Forces Engage in a New Kind of Training at Bragg," *Fayetteville Observer*, April 11, 2018.

Butler, Dwayne M., Angelena Bohman, Lisa Pelled Colabella, Julia A. Thompson, Michael Shurkin, Stephan B. Seabrook, Rebecca Jensen, and Christina Bartol Burnett, *Comprehensive Analysis of Strategic Force Generation Challenges in the Australian Army*, Santa Monica, Calif.: RAND Corporation, RR-2382-AUS, 2018. As of July 13, 2021:
https://www.rand.org/pubs/research_reports/RR2382.html

Carney, Stephen A., *Allied Participation in Operation Iraqi Freedom*, Washington, D.C.: Center for Military History, United States Army, 2011.

Center for Army Lessons Learned, *Initial Impressions Report—ARCENT Transition to Combined Joint Task Force-Operation Inherent Resolve*, Fort Leavenworth, Kan., March 2016. As of May 28, 2020:
https://usacac.army.mil/sites/default/files/publications/16-10.pdf

Chilcot, John, *The Report of the Iraq Inquiry*, London: National Archives, July 6, 2016. As of February 21, 2020:
https://www.gov.uk/government/publications/the-report-of-the-iraq-inquiry

Combined Joint Task Force–Operation Inherent Resolve, "CJTF-OIR Continues ISF Training Through Multi-National Efforts," press release, April 11, 2019. As of May 28, 2020:
https://www.inherentresolve.mil/Releases/News-Releases/Article/1811683/cjtf-oir-continues-isf-training-through-multi-national-efforts/

Defense Security Cooperation University, *Security Cooperation Programs Handbook*, Washington, D.C., 2021. As of September 22, 2021:
https://www.dscu.mil/documents/publications/security_cooperation_programs_handbook/security_cooperation_programs_handbook.pdf?id=1

Dempsey, Judy, "Germany Criticized for Its Training of Afghan Police," *New York Times*, October 15, 2006.

Department of Defense Directive 5132.03, *DoD Policy and Responsibilities Relating to Security Cooperation*, Washington, D.C.: Office of the Under Secretary of Defense for Policy, December 29, 2016. As of July 13, 2021:
https://open.defense.gov/portals/23/Documents/foreignasst/DoDD_513203_on_Security_Cooperation.pdf

Department of Defense of the United States of America and the Secretary of State for Defence of the United Kingdom of Great Britain and Northern Ireland, "Memorandum of Understanding Between the Department of Defense of the United States of America and the Secretary of State for Defence of the United Kingdom of Great Britain and Northern Ireland Concerning Reciprocal Defense Procurement," January 2018. As of May 29, 2020:
https://www.acq.osd.mil/dpap/Docs/paic/US-UK%20RDP%20MOU%20signed%2022%20Dec%202017%20USA003826-17.pdf

Deployable Training Division, Joint Staff J7, *Insights and Best Practices Focus Paper: Forming a JTF HQ*, Suffolk, Va., September 2015. As of February 26, 2020:
https://www.jcs.mil/Portals/36/Documents/Doctrine/fp/forming_jtf_hq_fp.pdf

DeVine, Michael E., *United States Foreign Intelligence Relationships: Background, Policy and Legal Authorities, Risks, Benefits*, Washington, D.C.: Congressional Research Service, R45720, May 15, 2019. As of July 13, 2021:
https://fas.org/sgp/crs/intel/R45720.pdf

Doll, Abby, Angela O'Mahony, Craig A. Bond, Samuel Absher, Jonathan Cham, Jennifer D. P. Moroney, Diana Y. Myers, and Max Steiner, *Assessing the Benefits and Costs of the Pacific Pathways Exercise Series*, Santa Monica, Calif.: RAND Corporation, forthcoming, Not available to the general public.

Dorschner, Jim, and Andrew White, "Quiet Professionals: NATO Special Operations Comes of Age," *Jane's Defence Weekly*, June 25, 2015.

Egnell, Robert, "Lesson from Helmand, Afghanistan: What Now for British Counterinsurgency?" *International Affairs (Royal Institute of International Affairs, 1944–)*, Vol. 87, No. 2, March 2011, pp. 297–315.

Farrell, Theo, "Improving in War: Military Adaptation and the British in Helmand Province, Afghanistan, 2006–2009," *Journal of Strategic Studies*, Vol. 33, No. 4, 2010, pp. 567–594.

Farrell, Theo, *Unwinnable: Britain's War in Afghanistan, 2001–2014*, London: Bodley Head, 2017.

Feike, Markus, "German Experiences in Police Building in Afghanistan," National Graduate Institute for Policy Studies, Discussion Paper 10-02, 2010.

Hallmark, Bryan W., Christopher G. Pernin, Andrea M. Abler, Ryan Haberman, Sale Lilly, Samantha McBirney, Angela O'Mahony, and Erik E. Mueller, *An Analysis of Alternative Approaches to Measuring Multinational Interoperability: Early Development of the Army Interoperability Measurement System (AIMS)*, Santa Monica, Calif.: RAND Corporation, RR-A617-1, 2021. As of December 22, 2021:
https://www.rand.org/pubs/research_reports/RRA617-1.html

Joint Publication 1-02, *DoD Dictionary of Military and Associated Terms*, Washington, D.C.: Joint Chiefs of Staff, November 2019.

Joint Publication 3-20, *Security Cooperation*, Washington, D.C.: Joint Chiefs of Staff, May 23, 2017. As of July 13, 2021:
https://www.jcs.mil/Portals/36/Documents/Doctrine/pubs/
jp3_20_20172305.pdf

Joint Staff, Director for Command, Control, Communication, Computers, Cyber, Department of Defense, Chief Information Officer, "Mission Partner Environment (MPE) Quick Look," fact sheet, June 18, 2013. As of May 28, 2020:
https://www.act.nato.int/images/stories/events/2014/cde/cde2014ra_2c.pdf

Judson, Jen, "US Army's 'Defender Pacific' Drill to Focus on South China Sea Scenario," *Defense News*, March 27, 2019a. As of July 13, 2021:
https://www.defensenews.com/digital-show-dailies/
global-force-symposium/2019/03/27/
defender-pacific-to-focus-on-south-china-sea-scenario/

Judson, Jen, "Reforger Redux? Defender 2020 to Be 3rd Largest Exercise in Europe Since Cold War," *Defense News*, October 7, 2019b. As of July 13, 2021: https://www.defensenews.com/land/2019/10/07/reforger-redux-defender-2020-exercise-to-be-3rd-largest-exercise-in-europe-since-cold-war/

King, Matt, *1st (United Kingdom) Division Capacity Building Overview*, briefing, January 23, 2019.

Lessons Learned Operations and Strategic Studies Branch, U.S. Special Operations Command, *Multinational SOF Planning Insights: Operation Inherent Resolve*, Tampa, Fla., April 23, 2015.

Maciejewski, Justin, "'Best Effort': Operation Sinbad and the Iraq Campaign," in Jonathan Bailey, Richard Iron, and Hew Strachan, eds., *British Generals in Blair's Wars*, Surrey, United Kingdom: Ashgate Publishing, 2013, pp. 157–174.

McNeill, Dan K., videoconference of interview with Bryan Whitman, U.S. Department of Defense, June 5, 2007.

Maldonado-Suarez, Ashley, "Exercise Talisman Sabre 2019: Demonstrates High Mobility Artillery Rocket System in Australia," U.S. Indo-Pacific Command, press release, July 10, 2019. As of July 13, 2021: https://www.pacom.mil/Media/News/News-Article-View/Article/1901005/exercise-talisman-sabre-2019-demonstrates-high-mobility-artillery-rocket-system/

Marquis, Jefferson P., Michael J. McNerney, S. Rebecca Zimmerman, Merrie Archer, Jeremy Boback, and David Stebbins, *Developing an Assessment, Monitoring, and Evaluation Framework for U.S. Department of Defense Security Cooperation*, Santa Monica, Calif.: RAND Corporation, RR-1611-OSD, 2016. As of July 19, 2021: https://www.rand.org/pubs/research_reports/RR1611.html

Marsh, Rich, "Joint Warfighting Assessment 2019: Seven Nations Meet to Finalize Plans," U.S. Army, webpage, January 25, 2019. As of July 13, 2021: https://www.army.mil/article/216613/joint_warfighting_assessment_2019_seven_nations_meet_to_finalize_plans

Mattis, Jim, *Summary of the 2018 National Defense Strategy of the United States: Sharpening the American Military's Competitive Edge*, Washington, D.C.: U.S. Department of Defense, 2018. As of July 13, 2021: https://dod.defense.gov/Portals/1/Documents/pubs/2018-National-Defense-Strategy-Summary.pdf

Ministry of Foreign Affairs of Japan, "Free and Open Indo-Pacific," briefing, undated. As of February 26, 2020: https://www.mofa.go.jp/files/000430632.pdf

Ministry of Foreign Affairs of the Republic of Latvia, "NATO Enhanced Forward Presence," briefing slide, July 25, 2019. As of February 26, 2020:
https://www.mfa.gov.lv/en/policy/security-policy/
nato-enhanced-forward-presence

Moroney, Jennifer D. P., Celeste Ward Gventer, Stephanie Pezard, and Laurence Smallman, *Lessons from U.S. Allies in Security Cooperation with Third Countries: The Cases of Australia, France, and the United Kingdom*, Santa Monica, Calif.: RAND Corporation, TR-972-AF, 2011. As of July 19, 2021:

https://www.rand.org/pubs/technical_reports/TR972.html

Morelli, Vincent, and Paul Belkin, *NATO in Afghanistan: A Test of the Transatlantic Alliance*, Washington, D.C.: Congressional Research Service, RL33627, December 3, 2009.

Morrison, Bob, "US Army Joint Warfighting Assessment 19," Joint-Forces.com, webpage, May 19, 2019. As of July 13, 2021:
https://www.joint-forces.com/
exercise-news/23548-us-army-joint-warfighting-assessment-19

NATO—*See* North Atlantic Treaty Organization.

NATO Joint Force Training Centre—*See* North Atlantic Treaty Organization Joint Force Training Centre.

North Atlantic Treaty Organization, "NATO Enhanced Forward Presence: 4 Multinational Battle Groups," briefing slide, January 21, 2020a. As of February 26, 2020:
https://www.nato.int/nato_static_fl2014/assets/pictures/images_mfu/2020/1/
pdf/200121-MAP_eFP-en.pdf

———, "Interoperability: Connecting NATO Forces," webpage, last updated March 24, 2020b. As of May 28, 2020:
https://www.nato.int/cps/en/natolive/topics_84112.htm

North Atlantic Treaty Organization Joint Force Training Centre, "Pre-Deployment Training for NATO Mission Iraq. New Task for JFTC," press release, May 16, 2019. As of February 25, 2020:
https://www.jftc.nato.int/articles/
pre-deployment-training-nato-mission-iraq-new-task-jftc

Office of the Deputy Chief of Staff, *Army Campaign Plan 2019+*, Washington, D.C.: Headquarters, Department of the Army, G-35/7, 2019, Not available to the general public.

O'Mahony, Angela, Thomas S. Szayna, Christopher G. Pernin, Laurinda L. Rohn, Derek Eaton, Elizabeth Bodine-Baron, Joshua Mendelsohn, Osonde A. Osoba, Sherry Oehler, Katharina Ley Best, and Leila Bighash, *The Global Landpower Network: Recommendations for Strengthening Army Engagement*, Santa Monica, Calif.: RAND Corporation, RR-1813-A, 2017. As of July 13, 2021:
https://www.rand.org/pubs/research_reports/RR1813.html

"Operation Shader: All You Need to Know About Britain's Fight Against IS," Forces.net, webpage, June 22, 2021. As of December 22, 2021:
https://www.forces.net/news/
three-years-op-shader-1500-airstrikes-against-islamic-state

Palazzo, Albert, *The Australian Army and the War in Iraq: 2002–2010*, Canberra: Australian Army, March 2011. As of May 29, 2020:
https://www.defence.gov.au/FOI/Docs/Disclosures/049_1617_Documents.pdf

Perkins, T. G. S., "Mitting in Basra During OP Telic 11—An OC's Perspective," *Royal Regiment of Scotland Journal*, March 2009.

Pernin, Christopher G., Angela O'Mahony, Gene Germanovich, and Matthew Lane, *Chasing Multinational Interoperability: Benefits, Objectives, and Strategies*, Santa Monica, Calif.: RAND Corporation, RR-3068-A, 2020. As of July 13, 2021:
https://www.rand.org/pubs/research_reports/RR3068.html

Powell, Alexander, Larry Lewis, Catherine Norman, and Jerry Meyerle, *Summary Report: U.S.-UK Integration in Helmand*, Arlington, Va.: Center for Naval Analysis, February 2016. As of February 26, 2020:
https://www.cna.org/cna_files/pdf/DOP-2015-U-011259-Final.pdf

Public Law 114-328, National Defense Authorization Act for Fiscal Year 2017, January 4, 2016.

Rashid, Ahmed, *Descent Into Chaos: The United States and the Failure of Nation Building in Pakistan, Afghanistan, and Central Asia*, New York: Viking Press, 2008.

Rayburn, Joel D., and Frank K. Sobchak, eds., *The U.S. Army in the Iraq War, Volume 1: Invasion, Insurgency, Civil War, 2003–2006*, Carlisle, Pa.: Strategic Studies Institute and U.S. Army War College Press, January 2019a.

Rayburn, Joel D., and Frank K. Sobchak, eds., *The U.S. Army in the Iraq War, Volume 2: Surge and Withdrawal, 2007–2011*, Carlisle, Pa.: Strategic Studies Institute and U.S. Army War College Press, January 2019b.

Ripley, Tim, Operation Telic: The British Campaign in Iraq in 2003–2009, Lancaster, United Kingdom: Telic-Herrick Publications, 2014.

"RUSI Interview with General David Richards," *RUSI Journal*, Vol. 152, No. 2, 2007, pp. 24–33.

Scheina, Carol, "U.S. and U.K. Armies Align Science and Technology Modernization Plans," U.S. Army, press release, September 30, 2020. As of July 13, 2021:
https://www.army.mil/article/239525/u_s_and_u_k_armies_align_science_and_technology_modernization_plans

Schüßler, Constantin, and Yee-Kuang Heng, "The Bundeswehr and the Kunduz Airstrike 4 September 2009: Germany's Post-Heroic Moment?" *European Security*, Vol. 22, No. 3, August 2013, pp. 355–375.

Serafino, Nina M., *Security Assistance Reform: "Section 1206" Background and Issues for Congress*, Washington, D.C.: Congressional Research Service, RS22855, December 8, 2014.

Serena, Chad C., Isaac R. Porche III, Joel B. Predd, Jan Osburg, and Brad Lossing, *Lessons Learned from the Afghan Mission Network: Developing a Coalition Contingency Network*, Santa Monica, Calif.: RAND Corporation, RR-302-A, 2014. As of July 13, 2021:
https://www.rand.org/pubs/research_reports/RR302.html

Sky, Emma, The Unravelling: High Hopes and Missed Opportunities in Iraq, New York: Public Affairs, 2015.

Special Inspector General for Afghanistan Reconstruction, *Divided Responsibility: Lessons from U.S. Security Sector Assistance Efforts in Afghanistan*, Washington, D.C., June 2019. As of July 13, 2021:
https://www.sigar.mil/pdf/lessonslearned/
SIGAR-19-39-LL-Executive-Summary.pdf

Ucko, David H., and Robert Egnell, *Counterinsurgency in Crisis: Britain and the Challenges of Modern Warfare*, New York: Columbia University Press, 2013.

United Kingdom Army Directorate Land Warfare, *Preparing for Transition in Afghanistan*, briefing, 2010.

U.S. Army Europe Public Affairs, "U.S. Allies and Partners Work Together on TACET Initiative," U.S. Army, press release, February 10, 2016. As of February 27, 2020:
www.army.mil/article/162032

"US and Australian Troops Go Virtual," *Arms Technology*, June 29, 2007.

U.S. Department of the Army, *U.S. Army Interoperability Campaign Plan 2019+*, Washington, D.C., 2019, Not available to the general public.

U.S. Department of Defense Inspector General, *U.S. and Coalition Efforts to Train, Advise, Assist, and Equip the Iraqi Police Hold Force*, Washington, D.C., DODIG-2018-147, September 13, 2018. As of July 13, 2021:
https://www.dodig.mil/reports.html/Article/1632556/us-and-coalition-efforts-to-train-advise-assist-and-equip-the-iraqi-police-hold/

U.S. Department of State, "Georgia Train and Equip Program (GTEP)," press release, February 1, 2003. As of July 13, 2021:
https://2001-2009.state.gov/r/pa/ei/pix/b/eur/18737.htm

U.S. Embassy and Consulates in Australia, "AUSMIN 2017 Fact Sheet on the U.S.—Australia Relationship," webpage, June 5, 2017. As of May 29, 2020:
https://au.usembassy.gov/ausmin-2017-fact-sheet-u-s-australia-relationship/

U.S. Government Accountability Office, *Afghanistan Security: Efforts to Establish Army and Police Have Made Progress, but Future Plans Need to Be Better Defined*, Washington, D.C., GAO-05-575, June 30, 2005. As of July 19, 2021:
https://www.gao.gov/products/gao-05-575

von Loringhoven, Arndt Freytag, "Adapting NATO Intelligence in Support of 'One NATO,'" *NATO Review*, September 8, 2017. As of July 13, 2021:
https://www.nato.int/docu/review/articles/2017/09/08/
adapting-nato-intelligence-in-support-of-one-nato/index.html

Waldhauser, Thomas D., "United States Africa Command 2018 Posture Statement," Washington, D.C., March 13, 2018. As of September 22, 2021:
https://www.africom.mil/
about-the-command/2018-posture-statement-to-congress

Waldhauser, Thomas D., "Statement of General Thomas D. Waldhauser, United States Marine Corps Commander, United States Africa Command, Before the Senate Committee on Armed Services," Washington, D.C., February 7, 2019. As of September 22, 2021:
https://www.armed-services.senate.gov/imo/media/doc/
Waldhauser_02-07-19.pdf

Walker, Amy, "Army Leverages Joint Multinational Exercises to Speed Network Modernization," U.S. Army, press release, May 1, 2018. As of May 24, 2021:
https://www.army.mil/article/204529/army_leverages_joint_multinational_
exercises_to_speed_network_modernization

Walker, Amy, and Justin Eimers, "Multinational Exercises Aim to Improve Coalition Data Sharing," U.S. Army, press release, April 8, 2019. As of March 27, 2020:
https://www.army.mil/article/219641/
multinational_exercises_aim_to_improve_coalition_data_sharing

Watts, Stephen, Christopher M. Schnaubelt, Sean Mann, Angela O'Mahony, and Michael Schwille, *Pacific Engagement: Forging Tighter Connections Between Tactical Security Cooperation Activities and U.S. Strategic Goals in the Asia-Pacific Region*, Santa Monica, Calif.: RAND Corporation, RR-1920-A, 2018. As of July 20, 2020:
https://www.rand.org/pubs/research_reports/RR1920.html

Welt, Cory, *Georgia: Background and U.S. Policy*, Washington, D.C.: Congressional Research Service, R45307, updated October 17, 2019. As of July 13, 2021:
https://crsreports.congress.gov/product/pdf/R/R45307/10

Westphal, Martin M., and Thomas C. Lang, "Conducting Operations in a Mission Partner Environment," *Joint Force Quarterly*, July 2014. As of March 27, 2020:
https://ndupress.ndu.edu/Portals/68/Documents/jfq/jfq-74/
jfq-74_44-49_Westphal-Lang.pdf

Wyeth, Grant, "Australia's Pacific Step-Up: More than Just Talk," *The Diplomat*, February 8, 2019. As of September 22, 2021:
https://thediplomat.com/2019/02/
australias-pacific-step-up-more-than-just-talk/